Inside Teaching

This book distils key research and evidence about what effective teaching means in practice. Covering all aspects of teaching, it encourages the reader to reflect on their pupils, their planning, teaching and assessing and their continual professional development.

Inside Teaching has an emphasis throughout on encouraging dialogue with pupils about what they're doing, why they're doing it, and how they can evaluate and develop what they do. Including questions for reflection and summaries of key ideas, the book provides practical support to help teachers ensure that they make a real difference to their pupils' chances of success. Chapters include:

- Pupils with different backgrounds and levels of support
- Working with your pupils' parents and carers
- Planning to frame your pupils' thinking
- Developing effective feedback for your pupils
- Making meetings useful
- Observing lessons and being observed.

This practical book will be an essential resource for both trainee and practising teachers who want to help their pupils to fulfil their physical, emotional and intellectual potential.

John Blanchard is a former independent consultant for schools, local authorities and higher education institutions. He was a secondary school teacher and has taught on initial teacher training, bachelor's and master's programmes in education.

Inside Teaching

How to Make a Difference for Every Learner and Teacher

John Blanchard

Routledge
Taylor & Francis Group

LONDON AND NEW YORK

First published 2017
by Routledge
2 Park Square, Milton Park, Abingdon, Oxon OX14 4RN

and by Routledge
711 Third Avenue, New York, NY 10017

Routledge is an imprint of the Taylor & Francis Group, an informa business

British Library Cataloguing in Publication Data
A catalogue record for this book is available from the British Library

Library of Congress Cataloging in Publication Data
A catalog record for this book has been requested

ISBN: 978-1-138-71228-7 (hbk)
ISBN: 978-1-138-71229-4 (pbk)
ISBN: 978-1-315-20026-2 (ebk)

Typeset in Melior
by Deanta Global Publishing Services, Chennai, India

For Jacky Blanchard, with thanks for wisdom and patience.

Contents

Contents

Acknowledgements

Thanks to Liz Worthen and colleagues at Optimus Education for working with me on articles, e-bulletins and training folders concerned with topics covered here. Many thanks to Steve Parker for reading the manuscript and making extremely helpful suggestions. Thanks too to Frank Newhofer for useful pointers. Gerald Hewitson helped me think through my main purpose and potential readership. Siân Tolba also gave me some excellent comments. In editing, Annamarie Kino made significant improvements to the structure of the text. I think this is a much better book for all their advice.

Many writers and researchers, whose names do not surface in this book, have informed my work. They include Erving Goffman, Dale Spender and Adam Phillips. I owe a great deal to headteachers, teachers, assistants, administrative team members and pupils in too many schools to list. Abiding thanks go to the following, each of whom has made a difference to who I am: my parents, Edith and Bob; my brother Ian and sister Maggie; my son Danus and daughter Gemma; John Ashwin; Charles Cuddon; Ray Ockenden; Keith and Marie Robertson; Tyrrell Burgess; Elizabeth (Betty) Adams; Ian Campbell; Mike Graham; the English department between 1977 and 1985 at Comberton Village College, Cambridgeshire, UK; John Pearce; Michael Fielding; Harry Torrance; Bill Brookes; D. Royce Sadler; Norman and Denise Schamroth; Mike Wardley; Daphne Wright and colleagues; Sue Hoxey, colleagues and pupils; Phil Silvester, colleagues and pupils; Ingrid Sidmouth, colleagues and pupils; Moira Bearwish, colleagues and pupils.

Abbreviations

ASDAN Award Scheme Development and Accreditation Network: a British charity organisation and awarding body, offering programmes and qualifications to develop young people's key skills and life skills.

BBC British Broadcasting Corporation: a British public broadcaster via radio and television.

CPD Continuing professional development: training, study and activity informing teachers', leaders' and managers' job satisfaction, performance and career progression.

CSIE Centre for Studies on Inclusive Education: an independent centre working to promote inclusion and end segregation in the UK education system.

CUREE Centre for the Use of Research and Evidence in Education: a centre of expertise in evidence-based policy and practice in all sectors of education.

DfE Department for Education: responsible for education, children's services, higher and further education policy, apprenticeships and wider skills in England.

EAL English as an additional language: having a first language other than English.

MIE Minimally Invasive Education.

NCSL The National College for School Leadership: a British government-funded, independent body for headteachers and school leaders.

NFER National Foundation for Educational Research: a centre for educational research and development in England and Wales, encompassing educational research, evaluation of education and training programmes, and the development of assessments and specialist information services.

Ofsted   Office for Standards in Education: the government agency in England responsible for inspecting schools and educational establishments.

SEN   Special educational needs: a classification referring to a pupil's requiring additional support.

SENCo   Special educational needs coordinator: person responsible for over-seeing provision and outcomes for children judged to have special needs.

SEND   Special educational needs and disability: a classification referring to a pupil's requiring additional support.

SOLE   Self-organised learning environment: what happens when people create conditions and ways of learning for themselves.

TLRP   The Teaching and Learning Programme: initiated in 2000 in the United Kingdom, funded by the Economic and Social Research Council and Engineering and Physical Sciences Research Council, incorporating 700 researchers in 70 projects, with researchers working closely with practitioners, covering all education sectors – from early years to higher education and the workplace.

UK   The United Kingdom.

Introduction

This book is about how to develop as a teacher in any kind of school for learners of any age. You may be experienced, newly qualified, training or thinking about becoming a teacher. My aim is to offer you ways to take stock, consider practical options, plan, experiment, reflect and still have time and energy to lead your life. I use research, practitioners' ideas and examples of policies and protocols to explore intuitions and experiences that make for satisfying and effective teaching and learning.

If you work with teachers as a trainer, mentor, manager, leader, appraiser, governor, trustee, inspector, administrator, parent or carer, I hope you will find here things to help you. I hope too that researchers will be interested in how I treat theory and practice, instinct and conscious purpose, in teaching and learning.

My emphasis is on dialogue with learners and teachers about what they do, why they do it and how they can evaluate and develop what they do. I build on some of my previous work, chiefly *Teaching and Targets: Self-Evaluation and School Improvement* (2002, Routledge/Falmer) and *Teaching, Learning and Assessment* (2009, Open University Press).

The book is a drawing together and distilling of my teaching, training and consultancy work over many years in primary, secondary and special schools. Most of the materials presented here have been developed for and used in practical sessions and projects and have been trialled and improved by teachers, trainers and mentors in their own settings. My intention is that you be able to pick out materials to chew over and adapt to suit you as you try to help your pupils fulfil their physical, emotional and intellectual potentials.

The book has learners at its centre and casts teachers as potential agents of change. Your core task as a teacher is to help your pupils learn as well as they can. The core task of leaders and managers, trainers and mentors is to help pupils learn by helping teachers teach as well as they can. The quality of education depends on how well everyone concerned with it contributes to creating environments that enable capable teachers to teach well.

Introduction

John Hattie (2015) used extensive analyses of educational research to conclude that: 'The greatest influence on student progression in learning is having highly expert, inspired and passionate teachers and school leaders working together to maximise the effect of their teaching on all students in their care.' In the BBC Radio 4 series *The Educators* (2016), the episode devoted to Hattie's work summarised his telling messages along these lines:

- A teacher's job is to see in pupils things they may not see in themselves.
- Teaching works well when it helps pupils try to do better.
- Every pupil deserves a year's growth in a school year.
- In excellent schools, teachers talk about the impact of their teaching.

Anyone who has tried to teach over a significant period of time must acknowledge that trying to live up to a specification like that is exhausting yet exhilarating, extremely difficult but worthwhile and rewarding.

Your focus is on your pupils' learning, so they take centre stage in Part I (Chapters 1–6). These chapters explore the effects of your pupils' backgrounds on their motivations, special needs, participation in what school offers them and their achievements.

Part II (Chapters 7–14) presents ways of working that teachers have evolved through conscientious experiment and study. These chapters illustrate qualities and skills that typify teachers who enjoy and succeed in their work. Topics covered include formative and summative assessments, planning sequences of lessons, home learning, the development of pupils' portfolios of their work and standardising formal assessments.

Part III (Chapters 15–20) examines wider aspects of what it means to be a teacher: effective collaboration, job satisfaction and enrichment, continuing professional development, lesson observation and appraisal. In conclusion, ten checklists are presented for key elements in your work.

There is a lot of jargon in education. I do my best to use plain English. Here are definitions for some fundamental terms, given with the understanding that other people may use them differently.

Checklists summarise things you and your colleagues have conscientiously to attend to if you are to enjoy and be effective in your work. Checklists enable everyone who is involved in key tasks to share decision-making, methods and responsibility. Chapter 20 presents ten checklists for major aspects of your work.

Lesson plans outline activities you want your pupils to engage in. I do not offer lesson plans, but in Chapter 9 I give prompts to guide your planning of lesson sequences. Nor do I quote examples of schemes of work or syllabuses, partly because you are likely to have those in your school through your own inventions and policies and/or through the work of publishers, commercial enterprises, curriculum authorities, examination and qualification agencies. I do explore the role of *schemas* in learning and teaching. You can use schemas to give shape and coherence to thinking you want your pupils to do. Schemas frame the cognitive work you want your pupils to tackle.

Progress refers to what your pupils learn; in other words, the understanding and skill they develop between two moments in time. *Attainment* refers to how well your pupils are judged to perform in tests, examinations and qualifications. *Achievement* refers to any aspect of your pupils' physical, emotional and intellectual progress and attainments.

Standards generally state, on the one hand, what your pupils aim for and, on the other hand, how good their achievements are judged to be. It is also possible to talk about *standards of teaching*, meaning, on the one hand, what you and your colleagues aspire to and on the other hand, how well you are judged to have done your job.

Criteria explain how judgements are made about your pupils' progress and attainments. Criteria can also be used to guide your efforts and to judge how well you teach and how well your school performs. Inspection handbooks, for example, publish the criteria that are used to judge educational provision and outcomes.

As a teacher, you belong to one or more teams, in name at least. Things teams are responsible for include pupils' teaching and learning in classes, year groups, subjects, departments and/or faculties; teaching of pupils with additional and special needs; pastoral care; cross- and extra-curricular provisions; resources and facilities; administration; finance; liaison with people and organisations outside your school; and management and leadership. *Team development plans* state how colleagues intend to examine how well they do, so that they might develop even better ways to help their pupils fulfil their potentials. Schools that focus on working as teams tend to be well thought of and successful. *Whole-school development plans* set the scene for and present a strategic overview of teams' development plans.

These are some of this book's main messages and implications:

- Your work is bound and led by laws, statutes and policies, but you are responsible for how you teach your pupils.
- It helps if you can share your successes with colleagues and speak to them when you have concerns and difficulties. The more of a team you and your colleagues become, the more satisfying and effective your work is likely to be.

- Working alongside and watching good teachers are probably the most effective ways to learn about teaching.
- What you achieve depends on what your pupils want to achieve.
- You have to value and use what your pupils know and how they see things. On that basis, you can enable them to fulfil their potentials through their imaginations, cooperative endeavour and study.
- Much of what you want your pupils to do is complex and demands persistent effort. The more positive you are about your pupils' prospects and progress, the better you enable them to flourish. Deconstructing the skills and understandings you want your pupils to develop can help you set up activities for them to enjoy and succeed in.

There is a big picture to attend to, but most of your time in school is taken up in the detail of interactions you have with your pupils and others who affect your work and your pupils' learning. Time and opportunities to enquire, research and reflect are crucial to your development as a teacher. So too are time and opportunities for you to be restored and refreshed. I hope very much you will be able to find here some of the things you need to help you be yourself and be useful to your pupils.

References

Hattie, J. (2015) *What Works Best in Education: The Politics of Collaborative Expertise.* London, UK: Pearson. www.pearson.com/content/dam/corporate/global/pearson-dot-com/files/hattie/150526_ExpertiseWEB_V1.pdf.

BBC Radio 4 (2016) 'John Hattie', *The Educators.* www.bbc.co.uk/programmes/b04dmxwl.

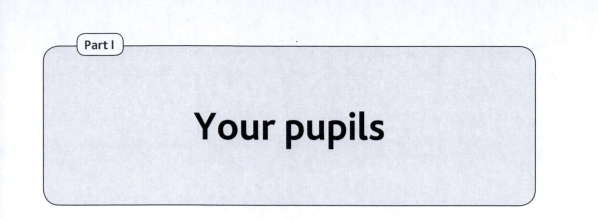

Part I

Your pupils

CHAPTER 1

Pupils with different backgrounds and levels of support

This chapter looks at how the circumstances of your pupils' lives can affect their school experience. How pupils are regarded and treated by people around them has a determining effect on how well they learn and how well they do. Teaching can provide pupils with essential, differentiated encouragement, support, guidance and feedback. We will consider how you can make a difference to your pupils' learning in school.

What difference do your pupils' backgrounds make to their school experience and performance?

Your pupils have different socio-economic backgrounds. You cannot change your pupils' backgrounds, but you can make a difference to how they are treated during their time at school.

Teaching is an experiment. You cannot be sure what the response will be to your intentions, plans and actions. Your work does not start or finish neatly, and outcomes are ongoing, not always evident and open to a range of interpretations.

Independent variables – things you cannot control or influence – include pupils' being young or old in their year group; their position in their family; their medical history; and their parents' recollections of their school experience. Dependent variables – things you can set out to control or influence – include how you work with colleagues, pupils, parents and others in planning, carrying out and evaluating your teaching; the kinds of activities your pupils engage in; and how your pupils' achievements are recorded and reported.

A key outcome might be expressed as how your pupils come to feel about learning. The more confidently they see themselves as learners, capable of finding things out and achieving things, the more they are likely to enjoy and succeed in school. Another outcome might be the results your pupils gain in national tests and qualifications. The better you enable them to take their next steps in life, the more they will appreciate their time with you.

You can try to find out which dependent variables affect your pupils' learning. Will it be home learning activities or group work in class, self-directed projects, the feedback they get or …? This is far from straightforward, not least because there are so many overlapping and interconnected variables, making it difficult to measure the effects of changing any one or cluster of them. In essence though, that is the task you face: finding ways to make the best possible difference to your pupils' learning.

Pupils' low attainment at school is associated with low socio-economic status and high attainment with high socio-economic status. These are correlations. Low socio-economic status is not an inevitable cause of pupils' not achieving well at school, and high socio-economic status does not guarantee academic attainment.

Against the odds, a minority of pupils who do not have obvious social and material advantages does well at school. And another minority of pupils whose upbringing gives them considerable social and material advantages falls short of what they are expected to achieve.

What can explain those apparent anomalies? Research by Iram Siraj-Blatchford *et al.* (2011) indicated that encouragement, support and affirmation, shown through conversation and shared activities, are crucial. How your pupils are regarded and treated by people around them has a determining effect on their school performance. The people who make a difference to pupils' chances of success show they are on their side: they express interest in the pupils' well-being and prospects; they celebrate progress and share triumphs and disappointments; and they help the pupils plan next steps and new ventures.

The research shows that successful pupils, whatever their background, are helped by people around them who nurture their confidence and resilience. Pupils who are relatively unsuccessful at school, from high as well as low socio-economic-status families, have little protection against the risks and obstacles they encounter. Deprived of encouragement and support, they do not adjust well to school and they do not do well.

Four groups can be identified. Groups 2 and 4 perform according to expectations; groups 1 and 3 produce unexpected results:

- Group 1 are pupils whose academic attainments are higher than their low socio-economic status would predict.
- Group 2 are pupils whose academic attainments are as low as their low socio-economic status would predict.

- Group 3 are pupils whose academic attainments are lower than their high socio-economic status would predict.
- Group 4 are pupils whose academic attainments are as high as their high socio-economic status would predict.

Pupils who are deprived of encouragement and support mostly have low school attainments. Pupils who are encouraged and supported by significant figures in their lives mostly achieve well at school.

	Successful school experience	Unsuccessful school experience
	Group 1 (better than expected results)	Group 2 (poor results, as expected)
Low socio-economic status	They have people in their lives who help them develop their interests and do things together; feel they can control aspects of their lives; cope with mistakes and setbacks; appreciate teachers who explain things well and are enthusiastic and approachable; adjust well to school and feel encouraged there; may benefit from additional or special provision; and view peers positively and learn from them.	They have little enjoyment at home and little continuity of support for learning; are left to their own devices; have a negative self-image; feel some people are born able to do things and others are born without those abilities; do not adjust well to life at school but feel it to be alien, confusing and unsatisfactory; are at best ambivalent about help that is offered and may be indifferent to it; and feel hindered by peers.
	Group 4 (very good results, as expected)	Group 3 (worse than expected results)
High socio-economic status	they have experiences that cultivate their sensibilities and give them a sense of entitlement; benefit from educational opportunities; and feel confident about their relationships with their peers.	They perform inconsistently; use ineffective learning strategies; make use of help when it is offered; are seen, and see themselves, as unable to learn easily; have little motivation to learn at school; lack emotional and practical support at home; say lessons and school do not work for them; and have uneasy and unproductive relationships with their peers.

Sugata Mitra ('Build a school in the cloud'; 2013) highlighted ways in which children benefit from the company of grown-ups who are not necessarily knowledgeable but who are appreciative and inquisitive. Mitra showed how 'admiration rather than discipline drives the learning spiral'. He called it 'the method of the grandmother'. Learners benefit from moral support and role models, someone to egg them on, someone to say, 'Wow! How did you do that?'

How can you make a difference to your pupils' chances of success?

Mitra's 'The hole in the wall' project (2007) showed that, given stimuli and resources, children can create self-organised learning environments (SOLEs). In the first of his experiments, carried out in a slum at Kalkaji, Delhi, India, children discovered a computer in a kiosk in a wall, which they could use as they chose at no cost. The aim was to prove that children could learn computing, among many other empowering things, by teaching themselves and one another. Mitra termed this Minimally Invasive Education (MIE). In addition to offering routes to qualifications and social mobility, it can be institutionalised education's purpose and function to help pupils to be autonomous, cooperative and fulfilled.

This is achieved in many schools. Damers First School in Dorchester, Dorset, the United Kingdom (UK), is just one example. Projects have included these defining features: continuity through the year-long projects; cultural resonance for the pupils; female and male role models; and enabling pupils to teach one another and others. At the beginning of one school year, two professional dancers, female and male, came to the school to teach a small number of pupils in each class, who in turn taught their peers. All of the pupils then taught teachers, assistants, parents and visitors how to dance the waltz, jive, cha-cha-cha .... The culmination in July was a 'Strictly Come Dancing'–themed celebration in the town's Corn Exchange. Another project was guided by a female professional film-maker. Scriptwriters, makeup artists, post-production people and so on came to the school and taught each year group about their work. Pupils then applied for specific jobs in their year groups, were interviewed and were appointed by their classes. Each of the five teams from Reception to Year 4 planned, wrote and made their own films. On a glorious summer's evening, the school took over a huge marquee in the neighbouring secondary school for the Damers world premieres and Oscars.

Compact examples of inspiring teaching and learning can be downloaded from the extraordinarily rich archive of, at the time of writing, over 80 pieces of writing by Chris Watkins, available via his website: chriswatkins.net/publications.

How well your pupils are encouraged, supported and guided in their lives affects how:

- prepared they are to meet the demands their school makes of them;

- open and flexible, rather than closed and fixed, their mindset is about their educational prospects;
- positive and productive their dialogue is with other pupils and adults.

With this in mind, you can try to make your teaching serve your pupils' shared and differing abilities and needs. You can provide your pupils with encouragement and support by:

- being inclusive and egalitarian;
- treating them in ways that balance challenge and support;
- being positive and constructive towards them and about their chances of success;
- negotiating ground rules and ways of approaching activities with them;
- enabling them to contribute to the planning, running and evaluating of their lessons;
- enabling them to work with partners in their researches and experiments;
- praising them for effort rather than ability;
- arranging for them to have audiences for their discoveries, performances and productions.

Your confident and well-supported pupils may take for granted that, with continuing backing and reinforcement, they can make progress. You can help their less confident and less supported peers to see that they too can make progress. This is neither sentimental nor false: children and young people can see through shallowness and pretence. They need hard evidence that they can do worthwhile and increasingly difficult things. In your teaching, you can add to the advantages your resourceful pupils already have. And you can do your best to enable your pupils who do not have those advantages to believe that, with help, they can try hard and do well at school.

Pupils in groups 2 and 3 are less likely than their peers in groups 1 and 4 to be clear about what they want to achieve in relation to what school asks of them. Pupils who lack confidence and/or social awareness find it challenging to fit in with others and assert themselves in healthy ways. Through your school systems and teaching, you can try to be sensitive and proactive about this.

Your aim can be to enable all of your pupils to enjoy learning. You can help pupils in groups 1 and 4 continue to develop capacities they already show, as listed in the right-hand column on the next page. You can help pupils in groups 2 and 3 to move in that direction and leave behind dispositions and behaviours as listed on the left (see Dweck, 2000).

Finding it hard to learn and do well, they:	Wanting to learn and do well, they:
Avoid challenges	Accept challenges
Take little initiative	Make suggestions and offer ideas
Don't look for alternatives	Consider different views and try different approaches
Make destructive criticisms	Recognise merit and criticise constructively
May respond for a while to extrinsic rewards	Do things for intrinsic satisfaction
Do not face up to difficulties	Are resilient
See difficulty as proof of being no good	Develop self-esteem through the ups and downs of experience
Blame or rely too much on others	Look for new strategies to try
See failure as proof there is little they can do about their situation	Stay focused on solving problems and achieving goals, no matter how difficult
Believe that success comes from in-born ability	Believe that effort brings success

You promote learning for all by recognising and supporting moves in the direction of wanting to learn and do well. To that end, you can concentrate on affirming your pupils' courage, initiative, determination, participation, generosity, flexibility and inventiveness, while being constructive and offering them ways forward when you challenge their lack of effort, evasions, negative assumptions and rejections.

Summing up

- Pupils who are encouraged and supported by significant figures in their lives tend to achieve well at school. Pupils who are deprived of encouragement, support and guidance tend to have low school attainments.
- You can try to make your teaching serve your pupils' shared and differing abilities and needs.
- Your task is to find ways to make the best possible difference to your pupils' learning. You can do that by giving them evidence that they can do worthwhile and increasingly difficult things.

References

Dweck, C. (2000) *Self-Theories: Their Role in Motivation, Personality, and Development.* Philadelphia, PA: Psychology Press.

Mitra, S. (2013) 'Build a school in the cloud'. www.ted.com/talks/sugata_mitra_build_a_school_in_the_cloud?language=en.

Mitra, S. (2007) 'The hole in the wall'. www.ted.com/talks/sugata_mitra_shows_how_kids_teach_themselves?language=en.

Siraj-Blatchford, I., Mayo, A., Melhuish, E., Taggart, B., Sammons, P. and Sylva, K. (2011) *Performing Against the Odds: Developmental Trajectories of Children in the EPPSE 3–16 Study (Effective Provision of Pre-School, Primary and Secondary Education).* Institute of Education, Birkbeck (University of London), University of Oxford: Department for Education, UK – Research Report DFE-RR128.

Your pupils' motivations to learn and do well

This chapter looks at pre-conditions for your pupils' being motivated to succeed and learn. We will explore how lesson activities can be made motivating and the roles that self-esteem, praise, peer influence, negotiation and shared problem-solving can play. The case is put for helping your pupils to regard themselves as partners in thinking about and influencing their lessons and school experience.

What affects your pupils' motivations to learn and do well?

Motivation is vital. Your pupils are bound to be asked to do things in school that they are not quite or not yet able to do, or not very keen on doing. If they will not risk having a go, they may not take on new understanding and skills.

Your job is to help your pupils try to succeed in what they do. They have to want to try. They have to mean to try. Then they have to try. It is that simple. And that is why your job is far from easy.

There may be pre-conditions for your pupils' feeling motivated to succeed and learn. It can be a prerequisite that they feel recognised both as individuals and as members of their class. You have a duty of care to protect them from harm and ridicule, and in the long run, the best protection is for them to develop, with your help, positive relationships in a constructive ethos. They want to feel safe enough not to feel disrespected or shamed and safe enough to take on challenges. They typically want to feel part of a group enough to have a joke and express what they feel. They also want to have enough time to themselves and have personal attention from teachers and assistants.

In societies and cultures that do not have young people's participation and autonomy as educational goals, pupils are not expected to play a part in thinking about what and how they learn; they have rather to comply with what is decided for them. But when pupils' voluntary commitment to their activities is prized as essential to their learning, your defining function as a teacher is not to represent authority but to act as advocate for your pupils' wellbeing and entitlement to opportunity. Once it is understood that young people develop constructive outlooks by having a voice and being partners in decisions about how they become involved in life around them, paramount importance can be attached to their motivation to engage with their school curricula.

The more your pupils feel they count, the more likely they are to respond positively to your encouragements and requests. At the beginning of a year or course, using name badges or a seating plan can help you address individuals by name. So too can using individual pupils' names as frequently as you can, for example, when you talk to the whole class. Being thanked and being told specifically what it is they have done well are powerful motivators for your pupils. It is difficult for them to resist wanting to repeat the experience as often as possible. And, of course the same applies to us all. One morning, arriving early at a school where I was doing some consultancy work, I came across the headteacher, Phil Silvester, and asked him where he was going. He showed me a list of names on a Post-it note: 'I have 15 minutes to catch these seven people before the day gets into full swing. I'm saying thank you to each of them for something great they've done this week.' It brightens everyone's day to show and be shown appreciation.

That is part of creating a climate in your lessons that can encourage everyone to feel good about getting involved. As your pupils come to know what to expect, they can begin to trust you. When they feel secure in the routines and relationships they develop in your lessons, they can be free enough to venture beyond what they currently know. At best, this can become a feeling of 'flow', as described by Mihaly Csikszentmihalyi in his extensive review of research into happiness and creativity (1991). Your pupils are motivated to be happy and creative when they enjoy what they do for its own sake. This entails having an uncomplicated sense of purpose, balanced with challenge, which sustains concentration. It means being absorbed in activity, undistracted by extraneous things and uninhibited by embarrassment or fear of failing.

A significant influence on your pupils' attitudes is how you regard them and their prospects. Many pupils come to understand that the purpose of education is to prepare them for life beyond school (e.g. see James Douglas, 1964; Wendy Keys and Cres Fernandes, 1993), and they are motivated by teachers and others who are committed to fulfilling that purpose. It helps if you model a can-do approach, and if you appreciate it when your pupils do the same. Optimism can rub off on doubtful pupils, conveying the message that success depends on effort. Without a belief in their own self-efficacy, they are unlikely to trust self-efficacy in others. Self-efficacy means being able to exert influence in spheres of our lives where we have some control, so that we are better able to bring about the futures we want and forestall the futures we do not want (see Albert Bandura, 1997).

Your focus can be on developing teaching that helps your pupils to appreciate that how well they do depends on how hard they try to achieve goals that are important to them. This gives rise to warranted self-esteem, as described by Carol Dweck (2000):

> Self-esteem is how you feel when you are striving whole-heartedly for worth-while things; it's how you experience yourself when you are using your abilities to the fullest in the service of what you deeply value ...
>
> When people have a contingent sense of self-worth, they feel like worthy people only when they have succeeded, and they feel deficient or worthless when they fail ... If you believe in the potential to grow, then wrongdoing simply becomes a problem to be solved.
>
> (p. 128)

So how you praise your pupils is important. If you imply they do well because they are talented or skilled, you condone a view of success as something some individuals, but not all, are born to. Alternatively, by your example and through your feedback, you can point your pupils towards valuing effort. You can try to encourage them to move away from thinking of ability as something innate and unchanging and towards thinking of ability as something that can be affected by many things and that can be developed. Seeing ability as fixed leads to helplessness or complacency. Seeing ability as incremental is a good part of wanting to sustain effort and achieve high standards.

One of the most effective ways of bringing positive attention to what your pupils achieve is to hold up and invite responses to their efforts in an appreciative, constructive spirit. Norman Schamroth at Damers First School had a delightfully straightforward way of giving status and credit to his six-, seven- and eight-year-olds' ideas when they were talking about things as a class: he typed on his keyboard some of the words his pupils said for everyone to see instantly on the interactive whiteboard, and the passages could be referred to later whenever it was helpful. It does not replace using an A1 flipchart or cards and Post-its on display boards, but there is something dramatic and formal about spoken words taking neat, visible shape on a screen as testimony to and record of individual and collective thinking.

Pupils can find their peers' responses and commentary more accessible and more telling than yours. Because they are so influenced by one another, it makes sense for you to give scope to cooperative as much as individual endeavour. One of your roles can be to facilitate exploration of feelings about what hinders and what helps learning. This can take the form of 'circle time' (e.g. see Jenny Mosley and Marilyn Tew, 1999), as well as other planned and opportunistic ways of finding out your pupils' perceptions and modelling how to be constructive.

In the informal setting of Sugata Mitra's 'Hole in the wall' project, children were in charge of what they did. In publicly, charitably or commercially provided education, it falls to you to set up and agree with your pupils how you will work together. One of your most important messages is that the class or group has more than one teacher. When they work together to share ideas, set targets, plan and carry out assignments, assess progress and make improvements, your pupils are teaching as well as learning.

There is little evidence that segregating under-achieving or demotivated pupils benefits more than a few. The ill effects of classifying individuals and groups as 'problems' or 'failures', and of depriving them of alternative models and supports, should be well known by now. The way you, your assistants and your pupils talk establishes a culture in your lessons. Most conducive to satisfying and lasting learning is a way of teaching described by Robin Alexander in his extremely helpful book *Towards Dialogic Teaching: Rethinking Classroom Talk* (2008). The main features are that talk is collective, reciprocal, purposeful, supportive and cumulative. The effects of these kinds of interaction are quintessentially motivating.

For Sugata Mitra (2007), children's motivation came from their curiosity about what an unfamiliar machine could be made to do and their shared pleasure in exploring and creating. The same can be made to apply in school. When children do things on their own terms, there need be no record of what they have done beyond their experience and the relationships they develop. In schools and other institutions, certificates and logs or blogs can play motivational and commemorative roles in their learning.

How can you engage with and guide your pupils' motivations?

You can ask your pupils from time to time to talk and, if possible, write in their own ways about how their work is going, for example, by using one-to-one contact times, planners, home–school books and progress files. Or your pupils can use a section in their folders or books to record their comments and ideas. It is good to speak when you can to individuals about what they write, and it is best not to mark this kind of writing in a conventional way. Do not let this become a chore – for you or for them. You can encourage them to be honest and to see this kind of shared reflection as a way of helping you teach them.

There are lots of ways of finding out about what your pupils find useful, enjoyable, difficult and off-putting. Here is just one example, which illustrates all of the principles referred to in this section. In a physical education lesson I visited, led by Tony Watson at the Queen Elizabeth School, Wimborne, the United Kingdom (UK), 13- and 14-year-old pupils were working in teams of six or seven. They took responsibility for:

- collecting and returning equipment;
- organising their teams;
- deciding which skills to concentrate on;
- how to pace their solo practising sessions;
- peer coaching;
- assessing their efforts by referring to agreed criteria (*confidence, accuracy and control*);
- observing from the sidelines and reporting on strengths and weaknesses in their teamwork;
- making judgements about how the lessons were going and how well they were doing.

I had the chance to talk to some of the pupils while they were off the court. I said to one pupil, 'I understand you gave a score out of ten last time for the lesson and your progress. Can you tell me what you gave?' He said, 'Six.' I asked, 'What could your teacher do for that to become a seven or eight?' He replied, 'Nothing. That's as good as it can be. He's a really good teacher, and the lessons are cool.' I asked, 'So why just a six?' He said, 'Well, six is as high as I can go in basketball. It's not my thing.' I asked, 'What is?' He said, 'I'm into street dance. I spend all my time doing it.' I did not have the presence of mind to ask him whether he was aware how the many things he was learning in these lessons contributed to his ability to pursue his passions.

It is motivating for pupils to feel they are partners in thinking about their lessons and school experiences. In some schools, pupils help change how lessons are run. In some schools, pupils observe and give feedback to trainee and newly qualified teachers, work with teachers to design sequences of lessons and carry out school council projects, for example, improving break-time arrangements, establishing anti-bullying policy and practice and creating and running school radio at lunchtimes and breaks.

There have been shifts in some schools regarding who makes decisions in the negotiation of teaching and learning, how decisions are made and where education takes place (see Donald McIntyre, 2003).

There are traditions and models of education that reflect such values and approaches, meaning that pupils' enthusiasms, questions and suggestions

Questions about how education can develop	Emerging answers
Who makes decisions about lessons and courses?	Less often teachers alone in isolation; less often prescribed or off-the-peg programmes; more often the pupils and others (e.g. teaching assistants, visitors, providers of particular experiences) in consultation with teachers.
How are decisions made?	Less often prescriptively; less often reactively, without consultation; more often collaboratively, explicitly and with a focus on how learning can be seen to apply in pupils' lives and beyond school.
Where does learning take place?	Less often in the classroom; more often in other settings (e.g. local places of interest, outdoor-pursuits centres, visits and projects abroad, further education college, work experience and training placements).

can contribute to what they do and learn. Whatever your pupils' age, they have a part to play in planning, running and reflecting on what they do. In the UK, the Royal Society for the Encouragement of Arts, Manufactures and Commerce's (RSA) 'Opening Minds' programme (2002) is an excellent example chiefly for secondary-age pupils. So too are programmes such as the Award Scheme Development and Accreditation Network (ASDAN), based in Bristol, UK, which has long-standing experience in forward-looking, pupil-centred education and qualification.

How hard your pupils find what they are asked to do influences how they feel about lessons. One of the obstacles to some of your pupils' taking part can be that they feel excluded by the manners and customs of school. For these pupils, school operates by codes they cannot crack or identify with. Basil Bernstein (1971) tried to explain working-class pupils' relative failure in school by their having inadequate access to language that would enable them to decipher and produce academic discourse. He constructed a theory for this, suggesting that middle-class pupils are familiar with language styles that he characterised as formal, abstract and syntactically complex. A weakness in his theory is that 'elaborated codes' can have shortcomings and vices as well as advantages and virtues: they can be unclear and over-complicated as well as articulate and succinct. Bernstein attributed to privileged forms of expression a lucidity they can sometimes lack. He described working-class pupils' 'restricted' language as predictable and limited by what its users take for granted. That seemed to prevent him from recognising that vernaculars can convey vigorous and rigorous enquiries and explanations.

William Labov is one of a number of researchers, teachers, historians, musicians, artists and others who have found creative, intellectual power in what appear to some people to be insubstantial, casual ways of communicating. He found parallels between some New York teenagers' discourse and Aristotle's rhetorical sophistication and showed how demotic speech is as capable of rational, critical expression as any elevated language form. In Labov's book *Language in the Inner City: Studies in the Black English Vernacular* (1972), the fifth chapter 'The logic of nonstandard English' presents a detailed account of young speakers' disciplined, forensic skill in analysis and argument. His evidence supported the view that 'There is no reason to believe that any nonstandard vernacular is in itself an obstacle to learning'.

Labov suggested we pay attention to what pupils say, as well as to how they say it. An implication is that, whatever your pupils' native tongues, your role can be to help them develop their expression and comprehension by using standard dialects, without excluding their own vernaculars. That is also a principle in teaching pupils whose first language is different from the school's, one example being English as an additional language (EAL).

How can lesson activities respond to and develop your pupils' motivations?

Language apart, tasks can be too easy, well matched to developmental needs, or too difficult (see Lev Vygotsky, 1978). Tasks that are feasible yet stretching invite engagement and effort and tend to motivate. Your pupils' interests can be aroused by surprise, novelty, puzzles and anomalies, and then extended and enhanced, when they:

- immerse themselves in activity;
- use their imaginations;
- learn how to find things out;
- express and pursue intentions and notice how others do those things;
- are taught and coached by enthusiasts and experts;
- work individually and in pairs and teams;
- pursue their interests and see connections between their interests and what they are asked to do;
- think about how hard they and others try;
- practise skills until these form spontaneous and flexible repertoires;
- see that mistakes happen and are useful;
- observe how others learn and are taught;
- apply knowledge and skills in real and as-if-real situations;

- use targets and criteria to help them judge their own, one another's and experts' efforts;
- see strengths, areas for development and ways of improving what they and others do;
- record their own achievements and reflections on their experiences;
- teach and coach others;
- give their view of how their lessons and studies go;
- explain what helps them learn;
- participate in efforts to develop what they do and how they learn.

When lessons have a healthy, affirmative ethos, your pupils are drawn into, and suggest for themselves, useful, interesting and increasingly difficult things to do. Motivation is sparked and sustained in activities that allow your pupils to express themselves and venture into new territory. These may be categorised as:

- finding out and exploring
- practising
- making and presenting.

When your pupils are *finding out and exploring*, they pursue what they want and what they have been asked to investigate. This helps them learn to work with peers and others, using diverse materials, media and texts, libraries, the internet, ways of coding, storing, filing and retrieving information … Curiosity and inquisitiveness drive these activities. The more strongly they feel that their quests have purpose and bring pleasure, the stronger their motivation and the more valuable their learning are likely to be. It can easily happen that you underestimate and underplay the value of your pupils' finding out and exploring things with one another and for themselves. Pressed for time and wanting to be sure they get things right, you may give in to temptation to tell them what they might better seek out for themselves, supported and guided by you, assistants and resources. When it occurs to you to present them with information, you might think again. What ways can you devise that are intriguing and enjoyable for your pupils to get information themselves?

When your pupils are *practising*, they try things out, make drafts or prototypes, repeat, revise, rehearse and train. This helps them learn how to inhabit sub-routines, techniques and processes that make up successful performances. Wanting to develop knowledge and skills drives practice. The better your pupils appreciate what their practising is for, the stronger their motivation and the more lasting their learning are likely to be. You may sometimes skip enabling your pupils to consolidate what they are learning in the hope they will pick up the routines that are involved when they need to. It could be better to try to think of appealing ways for your pupils to rehearse the knowledge and skill they have begun to familiarise themselves with.

When your pupils are *making and presenting*, they design, create, give a talk or performance, mount an exhibition, make a display or broadcast and teach. This enables them to learn about sharing what they know with one another and other people. Wanting to create and communicate drives these activities. The more strongly your pupils realise why they are producing and presenting something, the stronger their motivation and the more profound their learning are likely to be. If you are inclined to reach for a controlling strategy rather than risk untidiness and unpredictability, think again. Take a lead from what your pupils say and look for how your pupils can put their learning to practical, possibly entertaining use.

You can structure your pupils' units and topics so that they initially find out and explore things, then practise and make things and, finally, produce and present things. But interweaving and spiralling the different kinds of activity can make a powerful difference to your pupils' learning. For example, it can be very valuable for them to research or have a first go at something on their own and then give a short, informal presentation. They might tell the class what they found out by searching the internet or talking to family members. They might work in twos, threes or fours to decide how to read aloud a play script or text, then present it to the class. They might try out a skill in pairs or small teams and then show the class. Having an immediate purpose and audience brings focus, urgency and pride to what they do. None of this is unusual if you have an approach to teaching that relies on much more than the transmission of information and regular testing. The benefits are at least twofold: your pupils have more time and different contexts to familiarise themselves with what they are dealing with; and their confidence and skill levels are likely to increase with recursive activities.

Here is an example of such teaching which I saw when visiting Kate Hairs' mathematics department at Twynham School, Christchurch, UK around 1990 when 16+ examinations were being reformed and tests were being thought about for pupils at 11+ and 14+. A class of 11- and 12-old pupils, representing a wide range of abilities and needs, was working keenly in groups of three, four or five on a particular problem. There was a feeling in the room that they were all getting somewhere. Ten minutes or so before the end of the lesson their teacher, Ann Miller, asked a group to present their findings, and they did. Their fellow pupils appreciated what they had done. A second group was asked to step up. And so on. Ann had shrewdly sequenced the group presentations to show a progression in the complexity of ideas. By the end, we were all up to speed with alternative working methods, the last of which was most elegant. Everyone had played their part. We had all followed the same learning path, constructed by the pupils themselves.

Above all, education becomes motivating for pupils when what they express and show interest in is taken seriously, responded to and acted on. When teaching touches pupils' interests, matches their abilities and meets their needs, school plays a vital part in creating healthy and resourceful communities.

See checklist C5 on page 160.

Summing up

- To become constructive contributors to their communities, your pupils have to learn how satisfying it can be to play a part in decisions about their activities.

- The more your pupils feel they matter, the more likely they are to respond positively to your encouragements and requests. As your pupils come to know what to expect in your lessons, they can begin to trust you.

- Motivation and engagement are sparked and sustained in activities that allow your pupils to express themselves and venture into new territory. These can be summarised as finding out and exploring; practising; and making and presenting.

- It helps if you model a can-do approach and show your appreciation when your pupils do the same. Optimism can rub off on doubtful pupils, conveying the message that success depends on effort.

- Seeing ability as fixed leads to helplessness or complacency. Seeing ability as incremental is a good part of wanting to sustain effort and achieve high standards.

- Education becomes motivating for pupils when what they show interest in is taken seriously, responded to and acted on.

- To become constructive contributors to their communities, your pupils have to learn how satisfying it can be to play a part in decisions about their activities.

References

Alexander, R. (2008) *Towards Dialogic Teaching: Rethinking Classroom Talk*. York, UK: The University of York.

Award Scheme Development and Accreditation Network (ASDAN).

Bandura, A. (1997) *Self-Efficacy: The Exercise of Control*. New York: WH Freeman and Co.

Part I: Your pupils

Bernstein, B. (1971) *Class, Codes and Control: Theoretical Studies Towards a Sociology of Language.* London, UK: Routledge & Kegan Paul.

Csikszentmihalyi, M. (1991) *Flow: The Psychology of Optimal Experience.* New York: Harper Collins.

Douglas, J. W. B. (1964) *The Home and the School: A Study of Ability and Attainment in the Primary Schools.* London, UK: MacGibbon and Kee.

Dweck, C. (2000) *Self-Theories: Their Role in Motivation, Personality, and Development.* Philadelphia, PA: Psychology Press.

Keys, W. and Fernandes, C. (1993) *What do students think about school: Research into the factors associated with positive and negative attitudes to school and education.* Slough: National Foundation for Educational Research.

Labov, W. (1972) *Language in the Inner City: Studies in the Black English Vernacular.* Philadelphia, PA: University of Pennsylvania Press.

McIntyre, D. (2003) 'Has classroom teaching served its day?' in Melanie Nind and colleagues, *Inclusive Education: Diverse Perspectives.* Abingdon, UK: David Fulton.

Mitra, S. (2007) 'The hole in the wall'. https://www.ted.com/talks/sugata_mitra_shows_how_kids_teach_themselves?language=en.

Mosley, J. and Tew, M. (1999) *Quality Circle Time in the Secondary School: A Handbook of Good Practice.* Abingdon, UK: David Fulton.

Royal Society for the Encouragement of Arts, Manufactures and Commerce (2002) 'Opening Minds' programme.

Vygotsky, L. (1978) *Mind in Society: the Development of Higher Psychological Processes.* Cambridge, MA: Harvard University Press.

Thinking about what your pupils can achieve

This chapter uses a typical chances chart to illustrate the role performance data can have in framing expectations for your pupils' academic performance. Combining information about your pupils' statistically calculated prospects with your understanding of them as unique individuals, you can choose and develop materials and methods to promote your pupils' learning. Sources of data will be explained and attention given to how your team's effectiveness can be reviewed and worked on to benefit everyone.

How can statistics help you gauge what your pupils can achieve?

Your pupils come to school with different experiences, abilities and needs. They have their own ways of responding to your teaching. They do not learn at the same rate. Their achievements cover any number of spectrums. You have always to try to take account of their unique personalities and situations.

Whatever expectations you may have of your pupils' academic performance based on what you know about them as individuals and their backgrounds, you can also make use of systematically collected data about very large numbers of comparable pupils' academic performance. Past pupils' trajectories from common starting points indicate how well your pupils might do. For example, points scored in baseline assessments carried out in your pupils' reception class can be used to predict their performance at 7+. Points awarded at 7+ anticipate what they might do at 11+. What happens at 11+ points to 16+ scores, which in turn can forecast results at 18+.

You may be able to use data for national cohorts over recent times relating to two sets of assessments: those your pupils have taken before they come to you, and those your pupils will go on to take while you are teaching them or when they leave you, indicating chances like these.

Of course, chances are not guarantees. Statistical projections do not determine or set limits on what your pupils achieve. You can do better than set

Pupils with these scores before they come to you ...	... have these chances in their next assessment
<11	11% chance of scoring <10
	25% chance of scoring 11–14
	45% chance of scoring 15–20
	19% chance of scoring >20
11–20	15% chance of scoring 5–20
	17% chance of scoring 21–24
	58% chance of scoring 25–29
	10% chance of scoring >29
>20	6% chance of scoring <21
	17% chance of scoring 21–27
	56% chance of scoring 28–29
	21% chance of scoring >29

expectations and targets for your pupils based on attainment data alone. You and your pupils can try at least to match indicative success and surpass predicted average or poor performance. Ian Schagen (2000) reminded us that statistics do not give good answers to questions about why pupils and schools perform as they do. When you frame ideas about what your pupils might achieve and how you might teach them, it makes sense to use what you know of your pupils and what you know about teaching and learning, alongside statistical data. As Schagen wrote:

> Statistics always refuse to say anything about their causality ... Good statistical analysis can give us the crucial insights to develop theories, to support them, and to reject the ones that are out of line with the data ... Any educational theory or suggested intervention whose results cannot be measured in some way should be regarded with suspicion. If it really works, it should be possible to see the results in the numbers – somehow or somewhere.
>
> (2000, p. 97)

You can be aware that there are no panaceas, because individuals and circumstances are infinitely variable and changing. You want to know whether these methods and materials help your pupils make good progress. You want to know why certain activities enable these pupils to make good progress, but not those pupils. You can investigate why one group exceeds what the data predicted, why another group matches their predicted results and why a third group falls short. For the purposes of making comparisons, these can be treated as groups: girls; boys; pupils with special needs; high-performing pupils; pupils whose first language is not the language mostly used in your school; pupils who do not live with the family they were born into; pupils with different socio-economic statuses; and in fact any group that you identify as being of particular interest.

Getting to know your pupils as unique individuals and being aware of their statistically calculated prospects, you can take an action research approach to your teaching. This entails trialling methods that you have reason to believe could make a difference to your pupils.

This perspective has much in common with, and may have its roots in, the American school of pragmatism. Louis Menand (2001) gave a Pulitzer Prize–winning account of their work: chief amongst them in the nineteenth century were the philosopher Charles Sanders Peirce, lawyer Oliver Wendell Holmes, philosopher and psychologist William James and, later, educationist John Dewey. They emphasised treating all things human on a case-by-case basis, paying attention to what is particular about people and their contexts.

Action research derives from such thinking. Psychologist Kurt Lewin (born 1890 in Poland, died 1947 in the United States), for example, was a pioneer in exploring how to develop working capability in many fields. His contribution to human and social sciences has been well summarised by Clem Adelman (1993). Seen in this way, teaching becomes *applied research* and *practical theorising* (Michael Polanyi, 1958). It has been called *systematic self-critical enquiry* (Lawrence Stenhouse, 1981), *reflective practice enquiry* (Donald Schön, 1983) and, in its general applications to work contexts, *action learning* (Reg Revans, 1988). Andrew Pollard and contributors (2008 and 2014) have brought together a wealth of enlightening, useful examples of how researching teachers and teaching researchers have used enquiry and evidence to inform professional understanding and practice.

How can you use annual reviews of year-groups' performance to develop your teaching?

Working with colleagues, you can make use of quantitative and qualitative data. Keep in mind two questions: *How well do your pupils do? Do they do well enough?* Learn lessons from a single year's results but also look beyond them. Look at strengths, improvements and trends. Sources of data are:

- your year group's, subject team's and school's databases and analyses;
- reports about schools' performance in your network, area and nationally;

- publication and statistical treatments of examination data, including contextualised value-added measures and matching your school with others like it in terms of intake and type, for example, as provided by Fisher Family Trust in England and Wales;
- comparative surveys of pupils' attitudes, for example, as provided by Education Survey & Research Service or the National Foundation for Educational Research (NFER) in the United Kingdom.

Your own and your teaching team's effectiveness can be judged in terms of how well:

- you fulfil your own and your school's objectives;
- cohorts and groups meet your expectations and achieve internally set and officially prescribed targets;
- pupils do in your class or subject compared with other classes or subjects;
- pupils' attitudes to their curriculum experience with you compare with their attitudes to other classes or subjects.

You can ask good questions about the quality of what you provide and the standards your pupils achieve, examine evidence, find the best answers you can and apply what you learn. In some schools, teams take last year's review as a starting point and answer for themselves questions like these:

Annual review questions

What changes, carried out or continued during last year, do we think have contributed to improvements in our pupils' learning? If our pupils are not doing better than they have done in the past, what factors do we think are involved and what lessons are there for us to learn?

Are there focuses for development from last year that need to be continued? What new focuses should we prioritise now?

What do we learn from this year's review that adds to or amends what we have learnt in the past?

The point of annual reviewing is to benefit present and future cohorts. The more you and your colleagues understand how and why your pupils make good progress, the better placed you are to control things that you can control, and the more successful your pupils' learning is likely to be.

These are things that you and your colleagues can change:

- staffing of classes;
- how your pupils are grouped;
- how your pupils are consulted and involved in developing methods and materials for teaching and learning;
- resources and technology;
- activities your pupils have opportunities to engage in and technologies they have access to;
- in-house cooperation, for example, joint planning, team teaching, peer observation, moderating assessments and developing portfolios of your pupils' work;
- networking with other schools and organisations, for example, via local groups, assessment authorities and examination boards, subject and school associations and trusts;
- decisions about, and engagement with, qualification-awarding bodies;
- style and focus of continuing professional and team development.

Here is an example of how some colleagues express what they are committed to.

Values and aims of the .... team   Date ....

We strive to be inclusive: for example, arranging for a combination of mixed-ability groupings and groupings designed according to pupils' compatible capabilities; consulting our pupils to get their recommendations ....

We guarantee every pupil one-to-one time every term: for example, reviewing progress; providing additional or special support; planning self-directed projects ....

We work on developing our partnerships with parents and carers: for example, every pupil having one project per term to take home or work on in school club time ....

Here are examples of pointers some teachers and teams have used to guide their teaching and judge outcomes.

Objectives for cohorts and groups taught by the ....
team   Date ....

We are working on providing conditions that help our pupils speak up about how they feel.

Continued

> *We want our pupils to feel pleased with their progress and be keen to engage in self-directed projects. This applies especially to our pupils who have struggled with or not liked being at school.*
>
> *Our focus this year is for our pupils in Year _ to develop effective methods and materials for revision. We want them to learn about giving direct answers to questions in examinations: paying attention to relevance, clarity and succinctness in what they do.*
>
> *We will be successful when all our pupils leave us feeling they have achieved what they aimed for to help them in the next phase of their lives.*

Here are examples of focuses for development, emerging from performance reviews.

Developing provision	Promoting outcomes
Teaching assistants are concentrating on asking open questions and finding out from our pupils what they feel might help them. *Timescale: ....*	*We and our pupils' parents and carers will notice signs of increasing confidence in their talking about what they feel.* *Date for evaluation: ....*
Renew our curriculum for Years _–_ to build on our pupils' interests and project work. *Timescale: ....*	*More of our pupils will report they are very pleased with their progress and achievements.* *Date for evaluation: ....*
Discuss with other subject teams and senior leaders what changes should be made to the system of colleagues' logging termly grades for effort and achievement. *Timescale: ....*	*More of our pupils will talk about their achievements and progress and what they want to aim for in their learning.* *Date for evaluation: ....*
One of our team will be a test or an exam marker or consult markers and examiners, and will report to the team on what she or he learns. *Timescale: ....*	*More of our pupils will answer test and exam questions with relevance and precision.* *Date for evaluation: ....*

Summing up

- Whatever expectations you have of your pupils' academic performance based on what you know about them as individuals and their backgrounds, you can also make use of systematically collected data about very large numbers of pupils' academic performance.

- Your task is to ask good questions about the quality of what you provide and the standards your pupils achieve, to examine evidence, to find the best answers you can and to apply what you learn.

- The more you and your colleagues understand how and why your pupils make good progress, the better placed you are to make systematic changes to things you can control and the more successful your pupils' learning is likely to be.

References

Adelman, C. (1993) 'Kurt Lewin and the origins of action research', *Educational Action Research*, 1, 1: 7–24.

Menand, L. (2001) *The Metaphysical Club: A Story of Ideas in America*. New York: Farrar, Straus and Giroux.

Polanyi, M. (1958) *Personal Knowledge: Towards a Post-Critical Philosophy*. Chicago, IL: University of Chicago Press.

Pollard, A. and contributors (2002, 2005, 2008) *Reflective Teaching: Evidence-Informed Professional Practice*. London, UK: Continuum; and (2014) *Reflective Teaching in Schools*. London, UK: Bloomsbury Publishing.

Revans, R. (1988, 2011) *ABC of Action Learning*. Farnham, UK: Gower.

Schagen, I. (2000) *Statistics for School Managers*. Westley, Suffolk, UK: Courseware Publications.

Schön, D. (1983) *The Reflective Practitioner: How Professionals Think in Action*. London, UK: Temple Smith.

Stenhouse, L. (1981) 'What counts as research?' *British Journal of Educational Studies*, 29, 2: 103–114.

Helping your slow-learning and under-achieving pupils do well

In this chapter, definitions of *slow learning* and *under-achievement* are given, and their implications are explored. Short case studies of three learners with below-average attainment illustrate pupils' difficulties and a range of responses made by teachers and school systems. Spontaneous adaptations to pupils' difficulties in learning are offered. How you can try to dissolve learners' negative thinking is explored. Emphasis is given to the values of collaborating with colleagues and having supervision of guidance and support for pupils who learn slowly or fall short of what they are expected to achieve.

Why is it important to work with colleagues to help your pupils who do not do well?

Your aim can be for all your pupils to fulfil their potential as learners, physically, emotionally and intellectually. You and your colleagues depend on one another for this. Your efforts can be undermined if you do not have shared purposes and compatible approaches.

Your pupils' results in standardised or national tests and examinations yield probabilities for their subsequent performance. Projections can also be derived from experienced educators' knowledge of children and young people, their patterns of development and factors affecting their learning and achievement.

How well you teach pupils whose academic attainments are below average, or below what is expected of them, may be taken as a test of how well you teach. You may not be able to feel wholly satisfied with your work, and other people may have qualified respect for what you do, if the only pupils of yours who succeed are those who take school in their stride and achieve what is expected of them. This is not to suggest that all your pupils should attain above-average results and meet your highest expectations. We may have to remind ourselves and others that when you identify who is above average, half the population is described as below average; and that one of the functions of having high expectations is to set a bar higher than some find they can reach.

Any pupil might be slow to learn a specific skill or to understand a cluster of concepts. But *slow learning* refers to a generalised feature of delayed learning across a number of areas. It indicates that a pupil achieves less than is expected by a given age. Measured against approximate norms, slow-learning pupils fall behind their peers in academic performance, without necessarily having difficulties in their attitudes or motivation. Reasons for slow learning include impediments to physical, cognitive and/or communicative development. Programmes can be designed to assist learning and compensate for difficulties. Multi-disciplinary and/or multi-agency assessments may be needed. If specific barriers or disabilities are suspected or identified, a statement of special educational need (SEN or SEND) may be called for. Otherwise, you can try to match observant and empathic teaching with accessible yet challenging tasks for your pupils who learn slowly.

These are examples of very helpful books on two vital topics: Maryanne Wolf's *Proust and the Squid: The Story and Science of the Reading Brain* (2007) about dyslexia; and Simon Baron-Cohen's *The Facts: Autism and Asperger Syndrome* (2008).

Measured against their predicted levels, *under-achievers* fall short of the progress they are expected to make. Under-achievement indicates that something is temporarily preventing pupils from performing at their expected levels. Reasons include disruption to home life and/or changes in peer-group affiliation, illness, emotional and psychological difficulties and loss of motivation and direction. Any pupil might under-achieve at a difficult time in her or his life. If what is happening can be understood and responded to, 'normal service' may be resumed before too long. If difficulties persist, so might under-achievement, prompting investigation and intervention.

The ill effects for pupils of a school's and teachers' not attending to slow learning include frustration, disaffection or depression; social marginalisation and isolation; and reduced options in education and employment. The ill effects for pupils of a school's and teachers' not attending to under-achievement include loss of self-esteem; shame; alienation; anti-social or criminal activity; self-harm; exclusion; and restricted access to future opportunities. The ill effects for schools of not attending to slow learning and under-achievement include unhealthy stress; diminished job satisfaction; missed opportunities to learn about learning in ways that benefit everyone; wasted resources; poor reputation; and negative labelling.

From the learners' point of view, the benefits of having slow learning or under-achievement identified and responded to include increased enjoyment, achievement and confidence; positive contribution to school and community life; and good prospects in relation to continuing education and employment.

For schools, the benefits of identifying and responding effectively to slow learning and under-achievement include increased job satisfaction; public recognition; and enhanced development opportunities.

What might slow learning and under-achievement look like, and how might teachers and systems respond?

Here are short case studies of three learners with below-average attainment.

Nine-year-old Kevin has no brothers or sisters. His mother says she 'overprotects' him. His attendance at primary school has been excellent. His physical development is normal. He began reading and writing late and made below-average progress in literacy and most other areas of the curriculum. He has developed well in personal and social respects, being considerate, friendly, diligent and good-humoured. Since the age of 7, he has been on the SEN (special educational needs) register and has received one-to-one literacy and numeracy support in addition to booster classes. In lessons, he usually tries hard and has become confident enough not to seek repeated re-assurance. He can sustain concentration, particularly when guided at the outset on what to attend to. Through sheer effort, Kevin usually manages to achieve his goals; he wants to do well and enjoys seeing that he is making progress.

From Kevin's start at school, his slow learning has been acknowledged by all concerned. A coherent plan was put in place and regularly reviewed. His infant school class teacher monitored and communicated with colleagues and parents about his progress. They were keen for Kevin's voice to be heard. His mother agreed and supported strategies and staff members learnt how to help him succeed. Currently, he is given extra time to read text information; someone, often a fellow pupil, checks that he is clear about how to proceed with tasks; additional home activities are set, often scaffolding improvement to assignments he has worked on in class. He has a balanced outlook and a positive view of his prospects. He looks forward to going to secondary school and achieving his longer-term aspirations, which are to go to college and then work like his uncle in catering. The system and provision seem to be working well for Kevin.

Twelve-year-old Lyndsey has a younger sister and two older brothers. She has just returned to live with her mother and sisters on a trial period, having been in care for a third spell. Her attendance at five schools has been around 75 per cent. In her early years, she suffered a badly fractured arm and later concussion; otherwise she has had no serious illness. Social welfare agencies have been involved in Lyndsey's care and education. In her junior school, she was assessed to be at risk. Since her arrival at her secondary school, SEN provision has been made relating to Lyndsey's emotional and behavioural development.

Her physical development is advanced. Her academic attainments have been consistently below average. She did not take national tests when she was 7 or 11 because of absence. In class, she attracts attention and finds it difficult to settle and complete tasks. An intimidating leader, she experiences conflict with and disrupts peers. It takes time for adults to develop trusting relationships with Lyndsey. A number of her teachers feel that, if stability can be achieved, she is capable of attaining at least average results, though mathematics and science pose particular problems. Lyndsey already has a view of her future after college as a nursery nurse or nanny or working with animals.

Through out-of-class sessions, her secondary school SEN team is concentrating on helping Lyndsey to control her anger. Information about this is posted on the staffroom noticeboard, but Lyndsey's teachers are much more aware of their daily conflicts with her than they are of overall policy. Lyndsey has an unfamiliar tutor and a head of year who is new to the school. Attempts to introduce consistent approaches to her teaching, for example, via the student planner, have so far failed. All her tests (e.g. baseline assessment in reception, at age 9 years, in reading, in spelling, NFER-Nelson non-verbal reasoning, educational psychologists' assessments) place her well below average. This may be because in test situations, she performs below her potential, giving up or walking out. Whether she is a slow learner or an under-achiever or neither, Lyndsey needs guidance and support. None of her teachers feels they are 'reaching' her. A decision needs to be taken at senior management level about the school's approach to Lyndsey, her mother and the professionals involved in her care. Comprehensive investigation should lead to coherent planning. The help given and its effectiveness should be carefully monitored and regularly reviewed.

Fifteen-year-old Matt has a sister at university. He lives with his mother and has regular contact with his father. He went to an independent school before coming to his local 11–18 academy. Attendance overall has been average. He has shown talent for cricket, golf, chess and model aircraft, but he has not sustained these interests. By 14, he was reported to be performing at average levels in English and mathematics and most other subjects and at above-average levels in science, computing and physical education. His progress last year met high expectations. Early this year, he was reported for smoking and truanting. In class now he behaves erratically, often declaring lack of interest in tasks. Consultations with his mother and father indicate that shy and compliant Matt has become adolescent and part of a new social group out of school. He does no home learning activities, is withdrawn and difficult for parents as well as staff to talk to. His pre-16+ examination grades are towards the bottom of the range with some ungraded performance, except for a still worse-than-predicted top-bracket grade of C in double science. He has not discussed plans for his future.

Matt is under-achieving. This is obvious to everyone who knows Matt and is evident in tracking data. So far, standard responses by his tutor and teachers have met with little success. On the plus side, home and school are able to work together and his relationship with his science teacher is being maintained. An urgent start needs to be made to build on the positives. It is not immediately clear who will lead and coordinate the next steps, so this should be resolved by his tutor, the teaching team and senior leadership.

How can you help your pupils who find learning difficult?

Your first response to noticing a pupil is struggling can be to pause and observe, ask questions and/or adapt on the spot. Spontaneous adaptations include:

- critically reviewing what an activity is for, what it requires and how prepared the pupil is to tackle it;
- repeating, re-framing and/or improving instructions, guidance or support;
- slowing the pace;
- rehearsing pre-conditional skills and knowledge;
- introducing new resources and/or support;
- boosting resilience and ways of persevering.

When what you try makes little or no difference, more systematic enquiry and intervention are needed, involving communication with colleagues, further assessment and, perhaps, compensatory or special organisation and approaches.

It is difficult for learners to succeed when they believe they have little ability or little prospect of success. Until they are motivated to find a way around or through their difficulties, their learning will stay stuck. Effective teachers try to dissolve learners' negative thinking. An excellent source of information and inspiration for this is Carol Dweck's work (e.g. 2000) on learners' self-image and beliefs about ability. Another is the Centre for Studies on Inclusive Education (www.csie.org.uk). One important thing to work on is whether your pupils believe that the difficulties they experience lie inside or outside themselves. It can be the case that they do not recognise their own part in creating the situations that frustrate or upset them. It can be crucial for them to recognise what they can control and change.

Your school may receive funding to make additional provision for disadvantaged pupils. For example, in England at the time of writing, schools have to account for how well they use money such as Pupil Premium funding. Valuable lessons can be learned about what makes teaching, support and guidance effective. It is very helpful for staff to share approaches and strategies. If this has been missing from staff meetings or training sessions, time should be set aside for colleagues to learn from those who are successfully supporting slow-learning and under-achieving pupils. Mentoring or training for staff by teachers in your school and from other schools, researchers or consultants may also be useful.

The most effective response to slow learning and under-achievement is conscientious, collaborative and creative teaching, which focuses on high-quality teaching and learning for all pupils and is followed up with cycles of evaluation and development. One of the spin-offs of finding solutions to challenges in teaching certain pupils is that you discover techniques and strategies that benefit many of your pupils.

You can try to break down tasks into small steps; getting started can bring some success for your struggling pupils and unlock some optimism. You can say: *Look at what you have done well*, rather than emphasising what has not gone well. You can look for alternatives and encourage your pupils to do the same: *If we can't do it like that, let's try it another way instead.* You can prompt your pupils to identify what helps progress: *What do you think you need to do this well?* These are meta-cognitive strategies. The future will look brighter when your pupils find better coping and problem-solving strategies and when they feel they have begun to overcome some of their difficulties.

You can offer your pupils a prospect of things open to change. You can combine your thorough understanding of your subject content with being flexible about how to approach it. You can draw on others' experience and expertise to help you. You need lateral thinking, pragmatism and attention to individual pupils' responses and initiatives. You can focus, and encourage your pupils to focus, on locating strengths more than difficulties, exploring solutions and agreeing a plan of action to be regularly reviewed and updated.

Strategies to help pupils who learn slowly or under-achieve may be immediate or longer term, and include:

- pairing with a buddy or learning partner;
- providing a teaching assistant;
- periodic mentoring by an older pupil, member of staff or other adult.

The less success you have with spontaneous and short-term measures, the more you have to ask questions and discuss with everyone concerned.

Supervising additional and special provision is crucial, partly in order to be accountable for how you use resources and partly because there is much to learn from how you and your colleagues adapt your ways of working and continue to make discoveries about teaching and learning. The person leading and coordinating this work may be a tutor, pastoral or subject leader, special educational needs coordinator (SENCo) or member of the senior leadership team. She or he should do these things:

- provide information, guidance and support in relation to teaching pupils who experience difficulties;
- motivate and hold members of staff to account;
- give colleagues feedback;
- put colleagues in touch with one another to pass on experiences and expertise;
- develop an overview of how well pupils with learning difficulties do across the school;
- report to your senior leadership team.

Summing up

- Measured against approximate norms, slow-learning pupils fall behind their peers in academic performance without necessarily having attitudinal or motivational difficulties. Measured against expectations based on their own past performance, under-achieving pupils fall short of predicted progress, with attitudinal or motivational difficulties perhaps playing a part.
- You can combine your thorough understanding of your subject content with being flexible about how to approach it. You can draw on others' experience and expertise to help you.
- Strategies to help pupils who learn slowly or under-achieve may be immediate or longer term, and include pairing with a buddy or learning partner; providing a teaching assistant; and periodic mentoring by an older pupil, member of staff or other adult. One of the spin-offs of finding solutions to challenges in teaching certain pupils is that you discover techniques and strategies that benefit many of your pupils.

References

Baron-Cohen, S. (2008) *The Facts: Autism and Asperger Syndrome.* Oxford: Oxford University Press.

Centre for Studies on Inclusive Education (n.d.). www.csie.org.uk.

Dweck, C. (2000) *Self-Theories: Their Role in Motivation, Personality, and Development.* Philadelphia, PA: Psychology Press.

Wolf, M. (2007) *Proust and the Squid: The Story and Science of the Reading Brain.* London, UK: Icon Books.

CHAPTER 5

Working with your pupils' parents and carers

Research shows that more important to achievement at school than parents' social class or their feelings about how they did at school is how they routinely, spontaneously and thoughtfully support and guide their children at home. This chapter suggests that an essential component in effective social and welfare provision is trying systematically to see things from the viewpoints of those you serve. A range of contacts and meetings between parents and people in school can be beneficial if not essential. We will look at ways in which your school can promote positive home–school links.

How do parents and carers affect their pupils' school experience and performance?

Please, take 'parents' to include carers.

There is a consensus that parents prepare their children for enjoyment and achievement at school by the relationships and attitudes they have at home. Charles Desforges and Alberto Abouchaar (2003) found that:

> when all other factors bearing on pupil attainment are taken out of the equation, parental involvement has a large and positive effect on the outcomes of schooling. This effect is bigger than that of schooling itself. Research consistently shows that what parents do with their children at home is far more important to their achievement than their social class or level of education.

(p. 87)

Studies give examples of how parents' commitment to their children's wellbeing and development contributes to their progress at school:

- giving their children security, intellectual stimulation and a positive self-concept;

- contacting teachers and finding out about their children's school;

- visiting school to celebrate their children's achievements and discuss issues and concerns;

- participating in school-based community events;

- supporting teaching and extra-curricular activities in informal or formal ways;

- participating in consultations and decisions about the running of the school.

How can schools try to promote good cooperation between home and school?

Many parents want to see themselves as partners with you in their children's education. But some parents may not see you or themselves in that way, perhaps because they:

- leave their children to deal with school by themselves;

- have poor experience of schools and keep their distance;

- hold fast to believing that school personnel and/or other pupils are responsible for their children's not doing well.

Believing your pupils' parents are responsible for their children's disaffection and lack of success at school is a trap you do not want to fall into. An essential component in effective educational and welfare provision is trying systematically to see things from the viewpoints of those you serve. It cannot be overestimated how significant this is: not presuming or dictating to parents and their children, but learning from what they say and do, offering them constructive options and sometimes challenging them to take responsibility for what they do.

Your aim can be to work with parents' best intentions. You can support your school in trying to make a 'virtuous triangle' of parents, school and the wider community. Desforges and Abouchaar agreed with Linda Raffaele and Howie Knoff (1999) and Joyce Epstein (2001) that:

> Unless a whole-community, strategic approach to parental involvement is undertaken, and unless this work is embedded in the school's teaching and learning strategy and development plan, little return on effort can be expected. Outside this strategic approach, parental involvement activities tend to be ad-hoc, short term and to lack follow-through.

(pp. 89–90)

Crucial are contacts and meetings between parents and people in school and home visiting, when that is feasible and is thought to be constructive. Some schools have successful experience of fostering trust and cooperation between teachers and assistants and the parents of pupils with difficulties in learning, for example, via periodic reviews of progress, achievements, ongoing needs and prospects. In England, over some decades, there has been a legal requirement to carry out reviews with pupils who have a statement of special educational needs and, though it might be difficult to replicate that model with all parents and pupils, those arrangements show how precious an individual focus is and how personal contacts can benefit interactions with the parents of all pupils.

Because parents' encouragement and support is known to benefit their children's education, many schools try to promote positive home–school links in these ways:

- Newsletters.
- Catering for the needs of vulnerable children and providing facilities for parents, for example, offering drop-in sessions, general support, advice on health, help with emotional and personal issues, mentoring, financial management and flexible responses to expressed needs.
- Communicating with parents about support.
- Making referrals to and working closely with health and welfare agencies.
- Parent–teacher association activities, aiming for these to be popular beyond a committed minority.
- Informative and social occasions, for example, looking forward to coming to your school; considering options at 14+ and 16+; showcasing pupils' work; and preparing for transitions.
- Joint events and lessons for parents and pupils, for example, involving new resources and opportunities; showing assessment processes; and preparing for trips and special projects.
- Inviting parents to learn alongside their children and on courses that combine learning with leisure and other interests, for example, sports and healthy living.
- Pupils' involving their parents and others in home learning and extended projects.
- Meetings about pupils' achievements, prospects and plans.
- Up-to-date information for parents via your school's website and virtual learning environment, for example, clips from lessons and pupils' talking to camera to illustrate and explain typical and special activities.

- Consulting parents, for example, seeking their views via Education Survey & Research Service and responding to their suggestions.

Developing such activities can be a part of your team's and school's continuing development, and it might be something you take a personal interest in.

A superb example of multi-faceted partnership with parents and 'education with care' is Pen Green Children's Centre and Research Base in Corby, Northamptonshire, the United Kingdom (UK). This was the subject of an episode in the BBC Radio 4 series *The Educators*: 'The first teachers' (2016). We can share a vision of school as a fulcrum of the community, contributing to everyone's having a sense that learning is for them. Examples of this include the Cambridgeshire Village Colleges and Community Schools, established by Henry Morris between 1930 and 1959, and similar developments in Leicestershire and elsewhere in the UK and other countries.

Iram Siraj-Blatchford *et al.* (2013) have written fascinating and helpful case studies. Their conclusion was that:

> *the real world context of development is complex but while characteristics at broader levels, such as school policies and curriculum or parental jobs, exert some influence on children's day-to-day learning experiences, the best opportunities to help children are within reach right there on the near, every day, proximal levels. What becomes evident from our case studies is that unexpected academic success that defies the odds of disadvantage, requires effort and determination from the children as 'active agents' as well as from the people around them.*

(pp. 17–18)

Parents' and teachers' essential role in promoting children's and young people's successful learning is to help them participate in worthwhile activities and so become autonomous in pursuing their interests and contributing to their communities.

Summing up

- An essential component in effective educational and welfare provision is trying systematically to see things from the viewpoints of those you serve: learning from what the parents of your pupils say and do, offering them constructive opportunities, and sometimes challenging them to take responsibility for how they help their children.

- Your aim can be to work with parents' best intentions in encouraging, guiding and supporting their children. You can contribute to your school's efforts to make a 'virtuous triangle' of parents, school and the wider community.

- There are many ways of developing positive home–school links, and we can learn a great deal from research and one another's experiences and practices.

References

BBC Radio 4 (2016) 'The first teachers', *The Educators*. http://www.bbc.co.uk/programmes/b06s9j7n.

Desforges, C. and Abouchaar, A. (2003) *The Impact of Parental Involvement, Parental Support and Family Education on Pupil Achievements and Adjustment: A Literature Review*. London, UK: Department for Education and Skills.

Epstein, J. (2001) *School, Family and Community Partnerships: Preparing Educators and Improving Schools.* Boulder, CO: Westview Press.

Raffaele, L. M., and Knoff, H. M. (1999). 'Improving home–school collaboration with disadvantaged parents: Organizational principles, perspectives, and approaches', *School Psychology Review*, 28: 448–466.

Siraj-Blatchford, I., Mayo, A., Melhuish, E., Taggart, B., Sammons, P. and Sylva, K. (2013). 'The learning life course of at "risk" children aged 3–16: Perceptions of students and parents about "succeeding against the odds"', *Scottish Educational Review*, 45, 2: 5–17. Available cost-free via http://ro.uow.edu.au/sspapers/1187.

How your pupils can help decide what they learn and how they learn

Successful lessons and courses avoid making pupils passive and dependent and help them be responsible for what they do and how they approach learning. This chapter examines ways of collecting pupils' views about the running of their school and lessons and their suggestions about what could be improved. Pointers are given about how you can help your pupils play an active part in significant decision-making. A sample format for surveying pupils' perceptions is given.

Why is it important for your pupils to join in decision-making about what happens in their lessons?

You can treat your pupils' interests and choices seriously. Unwittingly and deliberately, they determine how effective your initiatives and interventions can be. It is healthy and productive to deal as openly as possible with how your pupils think and feel. You can help your pupils make decisions that are rational, recognising that rationality incorporates feeling. As they mature and as their relationships with you and one another develop, they can take increasing and more sophisticated control over their activities.

Chris Watkins, Eileen Carnell and Caroline Lodge (2007) and Chris Watkins (2016) defined such teaching as helping pupils to notice, talk about, review and experiment with their learning. They saw that teaching is fulfilling and empowering when it involves dialogue with and between pupils, promoting deliberation and reflection. This enables pupils to see that they can explore and create and so develop skills and understanding. Doing those things piques and guides their motivation. This is essential if, sometimes at least, your pupils are not going to be content with doing just enough to satisfy themselves or you – if they are going to stretch themselves. Your aims can be for them to see the point of trying, to experience success in their learning and to want more of it.

What kinds of things can your pupils help decide?

Albert Bandura (1997) showed that successful learners control what they can: things such as their attendance, attention and perseverance. They are motivated to do so when their feelings and thoughts are expressed in decisions they take about their activities. They can decide, for example:

- ground rules for how they work;
- what to aim for in their activities and learning;
- their priorities in activity;
- what steps to take to achieve their aims;
- what to do when they get stuck or go wrong;
- when and how to assess their efforts;
- what they and others are getting better at;
- how to improve what they and their peers do;
- how to apply what they learn across a range of contexts.

If they feel secure and are used to autonomous, cooperative and fulfilling activity in their lives outside school, very young children can decide such things instinctively and without much deliberation. When the need arises and as they mature, you can help your pupils steer activities by asking them questions like these:

- *Is there anything else you need to know before you start?*
- *About how long will this take to do well?*
- *What's going well so far?*
- *What do you need to find out now?*
- *Can you speed this up?*
- *Do you need to take your time with this next bit?*
- *Do you need to go back over this?*
- *Do you need more practice?*
- *Are you ready to share this with others?*
- *Are you ready to apply this in a new context?*

Here are examples of what you can say to your pupils when you want to promote participation and autonomy, together with illustrations of what they might say in response and an invitation for you to envisage how conversations might continue. It can also be a part of teaching assistants' work to prompt and support your pupils in dialogue like this.

If you say:	Your pupils might say:	You might say:
How do you want to do this?	*... Is it ok if we work on this together?*	*...*
	... We don't want anyone dissing anyone else.	*...*
How are you going to start (or keep on the right track, or bring this to a good conclusion)?	*... Can I look at the instructions again?*	*...*
	... We've got a plan for how to do this.	*...*
How do you know how well you're doing?	*... Maybe my feedback tells me?*	*...*
	... When I assess this, I'm looking for	*...*
What can you do when things go wrong, or when you don't know what to do?	*... I don't know. Things just go wrong.*	*...*
	... We'll check with ____ if we get stuck.	*...*
What's working really well?	*... I'm not sure. Do I ask my partner?*	*...*
	... I'm pleased I managed to ...	*...*
What's helping you?	*... I don't know what that means.*	*...*
	... Having a time limit for each bit is good.	*...*
How can you make that even better?	*... Perhaps if I tried harder to ....*	*...*
	... I'm good at ....; and I can improve by ...	*...*
How can you use what you're learning now in other subjects or outside school?	*... I know we talked about this, but I've forgotten.*	*...*
	... I can see how this will help me when I'm trying to ...	*...*

Approaching teaching and learning in these ways means you and your pupils share planning and responsibility for activities. This can extend to your pupils' specifying their own projects and advising on curriculum planning and design. Some schools allocate time for pupils to organise activities for themselves, including home learning. You can ask your pupils to prepare their own projects along agreed lines; some might be solo efforts and some joint efforts. They can decide, for example:

- *What am I aiming to achieve? What are we aiming to achieve?*
- *What help do I need? What help do we need?*
- *How do I want what I do to be assessed? How do we want what we do to be assessed?*

Some schools invite pupils to join working parties to review and devise uni of work that will appeal to their peers. All of this can be the focus of enqui and action research. It can be reported on in reviews and evaluations of your teaching and used to inform further planning.

What can you do to enable your pupils to take charge of what they do and learn?

You can help your pupils be clear about what they are trying to achieve, and you can help them take as much responsibility as they can for what they do. You can guide them towards developing attitudes and behaviours that bring them satisfaction. You can model constructive attitudes and behaviours focused on their learning and feeling good about their achievements.

This kind of teaching gives pupils opportunities to think about and act on questions like these: *What am I trying to do? What is the point of this? How will I set about it? How will I know how well I do?* For your pupils to be engaged in their activities, they must have a sense of their answers to those questions. Without engagement, their activities tend to be aimless and inconsequential, or they will be little better than merely compliant or obedient. As they mature, the more they are able to articulate their thinking.

Here are pointers to help your pupils engage in their lessons with you. 'You' can be taken to include teaching assistants and other professionals who play a part in your pupils' learning.

Your part in running lessons	Your pupils' part	Actual examples
1. You take quiet, informal opportunities to help your pupils be aware of what they are trying to do and how hard they are trying. You communicate as often as possible with individual pupils and small groups, praising and prompting, finding out what they think and feel ... You ask your pupils to talk about what they're trying to do and what it means to them.	Your pupils talk safely and as honestly as they can about what they're doing, how hard they're trying and what it means to them.	*This week A____ asked for help with fractions because, she said, she doesn't want to be confused by them any more.*
2. You make clear to the whole class what you are expecting and aiming for: for example, you display focuses or objectives; you refer to these during and at end of lessons. You try to set the scene for activities so that your pupils have hints and clues about what to expect.	Your pupils try to be clear about what they're trying to achieve.	*B____ and C____ said to their group 'This unit is all about why people do the things they do', and then they checked with me that they were right.*

Continued

3. You ask for and accept help from your pupils, for example, to choose targets, solve problems, carry out practical tasks, organise themselves …	Your pupils try to help you and one another.	*I asked one group if they'd like to organise the whole-class presentations; they were happy to take on the extra responsibility.*
4. As much as you can, you get your pupils doing things and talking about what they're doing. You embody objectives and assessment criteria in activities, giving your pupils direct experience of key concepts. You make activities relate to objectives, targets and assessment criteria.	Your pupils are interested in the point of what they're doing.	*At the end of today's lesson, we asked the class what they thought the main focus of their work was. Several answered rightly that it is to do with how, under pressure, one thing turns into another.*
5. You give your pupils access to examples of other people's efforts to achieve the kinds of things they are tackling: demonstrations, models and exemplars.	When your pupils need to, they refer to examples of what they are trying to achieve, whether these are film clips, photos, artefacts, writing and so on; or their recall of something they've seen.	*A group of pupils is exploring some books about science for younger children, wanting to find out what kinds of words and language succeed in clarifying complex concepts.*
6. You give your pupils time and help to work solo, in pairs/threes, as teams and as a whole class. You help them be aware of how it can be useful to work in different ways on different activities.	Your pupils take advantage of opportunities to work individually. They also benefit from peers' input and cooperation. They are able, in various contexts, to comment on advantages and disadvantages of working solo, in pairs/threes or as a large group.	*Sometimes, my pupils first work as a pair or three on a problem, and then each of them tries a similar one on their own. Sometimes they have a go on their own first and then compare how they've done as a pair or a three. They say they like working like that.*
7. You talk about how long activities should run: sometimes in short bursts, at other times with more protracted effort.	Your pupils try to make good use of the time available, keep on task and vary pace and intensity according to what they feel is needed.	*Today some of our pupils asked if they could have more time to improve their first effort.*
8. You ask your pupils to decide things for themselves: for example, what to aim for; how to organise themselves; what sequence to tackle activities in; which assessment criteria to prioritise, and so on.	Your pupils take responsibility for and initiative in what they're doing. Sometimes they run activities and projects for themselves.	*My class asked me if they could present their work to another class to find out if they thought the stories they'd created were as funny and scary as they were meant to be.*

9. You talk about effort with your pupils, encouraging them to see how they generate and control their own perseverance and resilience. You talk with them about what they can do when they get stuck or go wrong.	Your pupils talk about effort as a key to enjoyment and achievement. They have ways of dealing with difficulty, and they talk about this with one another. They welcome increasing challenge.	*One of our pupils told us last week that he'd concentrated harder than before and was pleased with the results his team got from their investigation. He said learning was exciting again, like it had been in primary school.*
10. You help your pupils make connections between lesson activities and things in their own lives that interest and concern them.	Your pupils see how what they're doing in lessons relates to things they do, and expect to do, in other subjects and outside school.	*Some of my pupils said they thought the work they do in mathematics, explaining their working, was helping them think about how they approached tasks in other subjects.*
11. Only sometimes do you use rapid-fire questions and answers. Quite often, you give your pupils time to think and ask them to prepare their answers, for example, by talking briefly in pairs or threes. You help your pupils see there aren't always quick or obvious answers. You make it possible for your pupils to listen to one another and work together on difficult and intriguing questions. You ask your pupils to come up with their own questions and use those to frame activities and projects.	When your pupils need to, they take time to consider how to answer questions and how good their answers are. They know they can try to build up to answer questions about key ideas. They help one another find better and better answers. They ask stimulating and constructive questions.	*Today, my class checked back over what they'd been learning in their current research activity. They decided they wanted a quick-fire quiz. I divided the class into eight groups; each composed three crucial questions for the quiz. After the quiz, we looked closely at a couple of questions that most pupils had difficulties with. They wanted the next lesson to follow that up.*
12. You discuss specifics in your pupils' performance and progress and encourage them to talk to one another in the same way. You prioritise successes and, when you focus on areas for development, you do so in concretely constructive terms. You ask your pupils to identify strengths in one another's performance. You ask them to explain their self- and peer-assessments in their own language, while encouraging them to understand more formal versions.	Your pupils decide what is working and what is not. They talk about specific aspects of their effort, performance, progress and satisfaction. They assess themselves and one another, sometimes using the language required by qualifications they are trying to gain. They refer to specific criteria to assess their progress and point to evidence for how well they think they're doing. They give one another constructive feedback. They use their feedback.	*This week, we have been asking our pupils to record in their own running records one thing they thought they'd made progress in and one thing they wanted to improve further.*

Continued

You show your pupils how they can describe their abilities: for example, in overall terms, when it's useful, using a scale (such as national curriculum levels or examination grades); and most often in terms of key activity areas and concepts. You present ways of improving as means to fulfilling intentions: *What do you want to try to do even better?* You ask your pupils to select and prioritise areas of performance to work on, sometimes giving them 'menus' to choose from. These can range from macro items to micro components of knowledge, skill and understanding.

If they feel disheartened, they tend to bounce back. They identify what they want to work on and how to do it. They choose both wide and narrow aspects of their performance and learning to focus attention on. They explain why they're working on the things they decide need effort. They use their own objectives as measures for how their performances and capabilities are developing.

I was pleased they were keen to work in their special study pairs to share their successes and ideas about what to focus on. The session had a good feel about it, and pupils left in very positive mood.

13. You ask your pupils to comment on how enjoyable and helpful lesson activities are. You ask them to suggest ways to make lessons more interesting and productive. You ask them to say what would be helpful for their learning in future lessons.

Your pupils make constructive comments about lessons and talk about what helps them learn. They look forward to helpful and interesting activities. They take initiative in and responsibility for their own activities and learning.

Our pupils have been making suggestions about some of the media texts they wanted to research to enrich the project they are working on. This has led to excellent sharing of different ideas because they naturally had different experiences and preferences.

14. You encourage, guide and support your pupils in collecting examples of their work they are pleased with and work they think shows their learning and progress. You help them organise a portfolio to share with others, including their parents. Occasions for this include taking some chosen pieces of work home at half term; hosting visits by governors, inspectors and other guests and showing them their work; preparing a portfolio to take to their next intended educational, training or employment destination; making presentations for other schools and organisations to illustrate what kind of school they go to; and preparing submissions for awards, competitions and applications.

Your pupils occasionally select examples of things they have done that they want to share with others and keep in some kind of archive. They use the work they collect in a range of practical ways to help them do things, such as to reflect on where they've come from and where they've got to, and to apply for courses, apprenticeships and jobs.

On Wednesday evening, our pupils were responsible for welcoming their parents and carers as part of a new format for consultation meetings. Parents spent less time than usual waiting to see teachers and a good amount of time talking to their children about the examples and displays of their work in classrooms and elsewhere around the school. An unforeseen benefit of this was that many parents reported that they got to know the school better as a place and what it's trying to achieve than they had ever done before.

How can you survey your pupils' perceptions to help you develop your teaching?

The more pupils play a part in the running of their lessons and school, the more successful their learning is likely to be. You can help them think about what they appreciate and what they think could be improved. You can collect and analyse your pupils' views, preferably alongside colleagues in your team and/or across the whole school.

Your pupils' feedback can inform your team's development and whole-school provision. Informal communication, systematically attended to, is as important as sampling by means of interviews, discussion groups and question-naires. Doing this kind of research can be part of teaching assistants' work, too.

Surveying pupils' perceptions using ten statements about lessons

You can talk with your very young pupils about how they feel their activities are going, what they especially enjoy and what they might suggest for future ways of working. When they are able, you can sometimes ask them to write their responses to questions or prompts. Here is an example. You might choose to use two or three questions and cover more on other occasions over the course of a year.

- Ask your pupils to give honest answers, which will help you do your best for them.
- Help your pupils understand the statements and how to respond. Emphasise that the decision for each statement is theirs.
- Talk with your pupils about what the time-words mean, e.g. *often* = more than once a week or in most lessons; *rarely* = maybe once in a term …
- Tell your pupils how you will use the results and discuss how they can play a part in developing how lessons are run.

Please, show what you think is true for you in lessons: 3 = *often*, 2 = *sometimes*, 1 = *rarely*, 0 = *never*. Put in the number that shows what you think.

1. We talk with our teacher/s about how we are going to work together, e.g. agreeing ground rules and other helpful things. ☐
2. When I start an activity, I think about how I am going to do it. ☐

Continued

3. I find out how other people have done what I am trying to do. ☐
4. I know how my teacher and I are going to judge how well I do. ☐
5. I think about how I can deal with difficulties. ☐
6. I get feedback on how well I do as I go along. ☐
7. I find out what I am getting better at. ☐
8. I find out how I can improve what I do. ☐
9. I collect examples of my work, and I look back over them sometimes to see how I am progressing. ☐
10. I think about how I can use and build on what I learn. ☐

Information gathered like this presents a picture of how pupils feel about lessons. It can be extended to relate to home learning. It can be supported by school surveys provided by Education Survey & Research Service. When your pupils see that giving their views affects how they are treated and taught, they find value in being critically constructive. The feedback you get from your pupils can affirm areas of strength in your teaching and indicate ways of developing further.

Providing rich sources of ideas and support, two of the strongest and most significant developments have been 'pupils as researchers' (e.g. see Michael Fielding and Sara Bragg, 2003) and 'pupil voice' (e.g. see John MacBeath, Helen Demetriou, Jean Rudduck and Kate Myers, 2003).

See checklist C3 on page 159.

Summing up

- Successful learners control what they can, for example, their attendance, attention and perseverance. They are motivated to do so when their feelings and thoughts are expressed in decisions they take about their activities.

- For your pupils to be engaged in their activities, they must have a sense of what they are trying to do, why they are doing it, how they can set about it, how well they do and how they might develop their skills and understanding.

- The more pupils play a part in the running of their lessons and school, the more successful their learning is likely to be. You can help them think about what they appreciate and what they think could be improved. You can collect and analyse your pupils' views, preferably alongside colleagues in your team or across the whole school.

References

Bandura, A. (1997) *Self-Efficacy: The Exercise of Control.* New York: WH Freeman and Co.

Education Survey & Research Service (n.d.) *School Surveys.* www.edsrs.org.uk.

Fielding, M. and Bragg, S. (2003) *Students as Researchers: Making a Difference.* London, UK: Routledge/Falmer.

MacBeath, J., Demetriou, H., Rudduck, J. and Myers, K. (2003) *Consulting Pupils: A Toolkit for Teachers.* Cambridge, UK: Pearson Publishing.

Watkins, C. (2016) 'Moving beyond "Shut up and learn"', *FORUM: For Promoting 3–19 Comprehensive Education*, 58, 1: 27.

Watkins, C., Carnell, E. and Lodge, C. (2007) *Effective Learning in Classrooms.* London, UK: Paul Chapman.

Part II

Planning, teaching and assessing

A teacher's repertoire

Vital to your pupils' developing confidence are that you care for and about your pupils; convey consistent, constructive messages; monitor how well your guidance is received; look for positive outcomes, while being prepared to intervene when things go wrong; offer your pupils strategies for dealing with uncertainty and error; match the styles of your questioning to your specific purposes; balance instruction with facilitating your pupils' self-directed activities in all areas of their learning; and capitalise on what your pupils know, for example, about computing. This chapter explores how you can develop the knowledge, skills and qualities that stand you in good stead as a teacher.

What qualities and skills seem to underpin good teaching?

Your strategies and behaviours reflect how well you care about and for your pupils. It helps not to take for granted how significant it is that you care specifically about their learning.

Madeleine Bunting (2016) made a critical analysis of the role that caring plays in health services and recognised the relevance of this to education. Most important, she said, is that 'care' consists of initiatives and responses born of empathic attitudes and insights. It is not a commodity, nor can it be guaranteed to grow out of training packages. Bunting said that providing care combines 'competence derived from rigour and emotional engagement with the individual' who is cared for. She emphasised that 'caring involves a relationship over time … . There has to be a moment of connection between the person caring and the person cared for … . It is not precision work; it draws on instinct and judgement … . The quality of care rests ultimately on a combination of training, organisational culture and the disposition of an individual and their personal motivation.' Its hallmarks are 'continuity, spontaneity and autonomy'.

Caring informs how professional skills and knowledge are applied and how mutual understanding is developed between carers and persons being cared for. Inspiring examples are neurosurgeon Henry Marsh (see his account of his work in the UK National Health Service, 2014), general and endocrine surgeon Atul Gawande (see his discussion of end-of-life care, 2014) and neurologist Oliver Sacks (see his autobiography, 2015, and his many studies relating to questions of identity and diverse conditions affecting the brain and central nervous system).

Marsh, Gawande and Sacks exemplify in their unique, brilliant ways one of the most significant qualities in caring professions. It is to convey to those you want to help that you have time for them. As a teacher, you can do this by being clear about what you need to know from your pupils, what you plan to do and what the time boundaries are. It is reassuring for your pupils to know that, even though you only have one minute now, you and they can talk later or tomorrow or another day; or that another person can be free to see them sooner if it is urgent. Availability and continuity of care and attention are crucial.

Underpinning your care for your pupils, and consequently their responses to you, is your developing ways of speaking and behaving that accord with the person you think you are and the values you have. Carl Rogers (1961) called this congruence *being true to yourself*. This illustrates how teaching is a sub-jective, consistently demanding, moral undertaking. Your pupils sense who you are and how authentic your words and actions are. The closer you can be to the person you want to be as their teacher, the greater confidence your pupils are likely to have in you.

Your pupils can feel anonymous and can see school as impersonal and indif-ferent to them. These are consistent challenges:

- how to create opportunities for one-to-one and small-group teaching;
- how to be efficient without letting procedures and systems stifle individu-ality, humour and warmth;
- how to give the calm impression that you and your colleagues are there to help and that there is nothing too unusual or too hard to do something about.

The UK Channel 4 television series, starting with *Educating Essex* (2011) and going on to *Yorkshire* (2013), *The East End of London* (2014) and *Cardiff* (2015), illustrates these qualities impressively. Each programme was filmed over a year in a secondary school and shows the leaderships' and staffs' relent-less efforts to do everything in their power to help their pupils be the best they can be. Another brilliant portrayal of school life is Nicolas Philibert's documentary film *Être et avoir* (2002) about a class of 13 4–11-year-olds and their teacher, Georges Lopez, in the Auvergne, France. An excellent account of young trainees' being helped to find their feet is Charles Hannam, Pat Smyth and Norman Stephenson's *Young Teachers and Reluctant Learners: The Story of the Hillview* Project (1973). All of these illuminate skilful caring.

Your pupils sense how concerned you are for their wellbeing. They recognise whether they matter to you, as well as whether you are able to take charge. They begin to have confidence in you if you:

- show you have time for them;
- have good knowledge and are enthusiastic about the subjects you deal with;
- are serious, but not too earnest, about things that matter, such as safety, equality of opportunity and fairness in the way you treat them;
- try hard to help them do well, which means helping all of them without favour.

Giving pupils your time and attention, having good knowledge and enthusiasm, treating everyone fairly according to their needs and abilities: these give as good an initial specification as any for how you might create conditions in which your pupils can thrive. These qualities are communicated to your pupils most directly in how you present yourself and how you interact with them but also in how well you tailor the rhythms of your teaching to what they need to learn.

How you present yourself

As a teacher and a facilitator, you try to prevent bullying and abuse, and you look for cooperation and kindness in your pupils.

It can easily happen that your pupils feel you are not speaking to them. Many of your pupils come to school to make and meet friends. Some pupils do not expect school to mean much to them. As the headteacher of the primary school in 'Akenfield', Suffolk, the United Kingdom (UK) (Ronald Blythe, 1969) explained, her pupils left their souls at the school gate in the morning and picked them up again on their way home. Your task is to find a way into your pupils' world and work with it. When you address the whole class, try to make sure there is a consequence to what you say, such as your pupils having to do something specific using your information. Look out for how your pupils respond and be ready to help anyone who is lost or goes astray.

Your aim can be to influence pupils who disturb or disrupt others by focusing attention on how some pupils succeed. You want pupils who do well to be an example that others try to follow. So you present yourself as someone who is there to help your pupils enjoy what they achieve and want to learn more. Your pupils can be motivated by wanting to help you and one another, so it is good to make use of the fact that you do not know everything and you make mistakes.

You can see your role as helping your pupils tackle the interesting and worthwhile activities you arrange and oversee. There can be a threefold dynamic in what you do:

- Sometimes you give them information and guidance in preparation for activities they are going to begin or continue working on.
- Sometimes you work alongside them as they engage in and reflect on what they are doing.
- Sometimes you stand back and observe how they are doing, which might lead to your giving them feedback.

This differs from a traditional, unilateral model of teaching in which you are distant or superior, handing down knowledge and expertise to your pupils. Homer Lane (1928) wrote about this as a teacher's becoming 'the brain of the group'.

Many pupils seem to respond well when they see that:

- you want to find good ways to teach them;
- you are prepared to be flexible;
- you are fallible but committed to helping them;
- you need to hear their ideas about how they might best learn in your lessons.

How you interact with your pupils

Your pupils are unlikely to do well if they feel they cannot succeed. It is a challenging discipline for you to reduce to vanishing point the occasions when you say, *Don't … ; You can't … ; That's not right …* and saying instead, *Please, do this … ; Can you … ; I'd like you to … ; What you've done well there is … ; What can be even better is …*

Teaching a class of pupils, there is a pressure to keep everyone together. A suitable image is that you are leading a group on a hill climb. To sustain cohesion, the group should go no faster than its slowest member. You don't want the fittest and strongest to be frustrated waiting for those at the back. You don't want the slowest to drop out. You want them all to reach the top, if that is feasible, or to reach the highest point they safely can.

It means talking with group members in different ways:

- encouraging this one, cajoling that one;
- recognising this one is getting hot, that one looks cold;
- talking with this one about how to lean forward, with that one about stride length;
- suggesting this one think about others, and that this one think about herself.

When teaching, you have to appeal to your pupils' divergent interests and meet their disparate needs. It means identifying your pupils' particular strengths and scope for learning and growth and giving them choices: *Who is making progress in this skill or concept, and to what extent? Who is not? What do they feel they need to make progress?* All of this belongs to formative assessment. And in a healthy, effective group, everyone can talk to one another and help one another achieve their best.

Behaviours that you may feel are forced or artificial can have positive effects on your pupils: for example, using pupils' names as often as possible and, as far as possible, eradicating negative and punitive statements. It is useful to realise that behaving in ways that help your pupils is something you can train yourself to do. Doug Lemov is a practical advocate of this. His book *Teach Like a Champion* (2010) and his workshops present a collection of behaviours that characterise the 'intentional and reflective craft of teaching'. These include:

- planning what your pupils will be doing as well as what you will be doing;
- showing your pupils how to behave by your example;
- capturing your class's interest to focus their attention;
- posting lesson objectives so that your pupils can see them;
- letting everyone know they may be asked to express their thoughts at any time;
- addressing an individual's off-task behaviour unobtrusively;
- showing your pupils that getting something wrong is part of getting things right;
- constantly checking your pupils are coping well enough with what you ask of them, for example, by moving around the teaching space.

The keys to this are that you:

- reflect on your experience and discuss successes and disappointments with colleagues;

- prepare your pupils' learning environment to stimulate thinking and activity in line with the purposes you have in mind;

- convey positive, constructive messages;

- monitor how well your messages are being received;

- encourage and guide your pupils, always looking for positive outcomes, while being prepared to intervene when things go wrong.

Rhythm in your lessons

Your aim can be to keep to a minimum the times when your pupils are passive. Giving your lessons a good rhythm helps you do this. There are two main aspects to rhythm: momentum and format for working.

This starts with what your pupils do when they come into your teaching space. You can help them become used to:

- continuing with what they have been doing in your lessons so far;

- reading, viewing or listening to something or collecting thoughts and preparing for what is going to happen next, say, by looking at what they have been doing recently, choosing questions they'd like to ask, getting out equipment, suggesting how they might tackle what they are about to do and so on;

- checking work they have done at home before handing it in;

- following up feedback they have just had;

- preparing what they are going to do in their home learning.

If it helps, you might sometimes also give them time for any of these activities mid-way through or towards the end of a lesson, helping one another, perhaps in a pair.

Momentum involves pace and direction. Your pupils do well when they feel that time does not drag and that they're aiming to do things that matter. Format relates to the kinds of activity your pupils engage in, for example, finding out and exploring, or practising, or making and presenting. This includes whether they work on their own or with others.

You can ask your pupils to speed up or slow down what they are doing. Speeding up encourages them to be more urgent about reaching a goal, to stop prevaricating or idling. Slowing down encourages them to look more closely, more broadly or more deeply, or to check things.

You can ask your pupils to stay with the direction they are already taking or change direction. Staying with their present direction confirms the value of what they are aiming for and the methods they are using. Changing direction signals a shift in aims or methods and so may require fresh thinking and more information and/or discussion.

You can arrange for your pupils to have times when they settle down to work on their own and times when they work intensively with other pupils. Such times might last for one or two minutes, ten minutes or longer, as long as it serves their learning. As part of your promoting concentration, you want to balance quieter, personal activity with busier, more expressive activity.

How can you help your pupils deal with difficulty and want to do well?

One of the skills you can be intent on developing as a teacher is analysing whatever might hold back your pupils' learning. In order to tackle this or that task, your pupils need to be able to do inter-related things. If they cannot pay attention, remember, repeat, and revise, for example, they are unlikely to do well in the long run. Capabilities that underlie doing well in school and beyond include:

- being prepared to join in and have a go;
- cooperating with peers and others;
- listening, observing and focusing;
- speaking, writing, computing and using digital communication media;
- asking questions, researching and, if possible, reading;
- reporting experiences and discoveries;
- defining problems and designing solutions;
- asking questions and being imaginative, organised and precise;
- sustaining effort and persevering through difficulty.

The better you diagnose underlying causes and factors in difficulties your pupils experience, the better you can prepare activities that help them develop essential dispositions and qualities of mind, such as curiosity, imagination, confidence, cooperation, tolerance of ambiguity, commitment, resilience and pleasure in achievement.

You can prompt your pupils to think about how they deal with uncertainty, difficulty and apparent failures. Help them develop strategies for when they are stuck and when things go wrong. Your advice can be:

- *Ask a friend.*
- *Check what it is you're trying to do.*
- *Look at examples you have of what to do and how to do it.*

Some classrooms have such tips displayed and, when pupils say they do not know what to do, the response can be, *Have you checked our list of the things to do when you're stuck?* You might also have pupils as 'go-to' people with certain areas of expertise. Some, for example, might be especially good at thinking through instructions, some might have strong vocabularies, some might be out-of-the-box thinkers ... Often the best person to advise is someone who has just done well what others are struggling with. It is morale-boosting and healthy for the group if the mantle of expert is taken by different pupils over time. You can have an eye on every pupil at some time having opportunities to help others through snags and impasses.

You help your pupils learn by helping them work through difficulties and build on their achievements. This is one of the most important things you can teach your pupils: focusing on the positive and the possible. In your one-to-one interactions with your pupils, you can use steps like these:

- Ask the pupil how she or he feels she or he is getting on and offer your constructive view. Invite her or him to talk about what she or he would like to do better. Ask her or him to describe what is difficult. Agree on a word or sentence that sums up what she or he sees is the issue. After that, transfer your attention to exceptional occasions when things are not so difficult. Keep this positive focus from now on, trying to understand what seems to help things go well.

- Concentrate on specific things that the pupil does well. Give feedback affirming how she or he has tried to cope with difficulty, and perhaps succeeded, for example, *Well done for spotting what's hard* or *It's great that you have tried to make things better by* ... These are not vague or empty words but strategic steps in practising analysis and resolve.

- Use a scaling question about the issue: *On a ten-point scale, with 0 being no progress because everything is too hard and 10 being perfect success, where are you now?* If it helps, use something visual, for example, a ladder or road, to represent the scale. Then ask questions about possible next steps: for example, *What can you do to move closer to what you want to achieve? What might I or others do to help?*

- Turn suggestions the pupil makes into tasks for her or him to work on. As far as possible, every time you discuss progress, make sure the pupil has something to work on that includes a focus on noticing *when things go well* and *what goes well*.

- Ask the pupil to update you on how she or he is doing and to use the scale. Ask her or him to describe as much as she or he can about when things go better or well, for example, the time of day, who she or he is with, what is going on, what she or he is doing, and so on.

- Reinforce the focus on what goes well, on reasons she or he can see for things going well and on steps that help to maintain progress or improve further.

When the time is not available and when it is not feasible to use all of those steps, you can choose one or two to clarify what you and your pupils are trying to achieve. The point is that you can model an upbeat, constructive approach.

These strategies reflect forms of pragmatic counselling such as 'solution-focused practice' and 'brief therapy' (see Bill O'Connell, 1998), which we adults can use to assist our own health and wellbeing as much as to inform our work with children and young people.

When do you use whole-class teaching, and when do your pupils work in groups or teams or individually?

One of the factors affecting how well your pupils learn is how you and they vary their working as a whole class, as pairs and groups, and individually. Such shifts to and fro can influence how well they sustain their attention and interest.

The commonest reasons for choosing to teach your whole class together are that you want everyone to have access to the same experience and:

- view the same demonstration or material;
- be an audience together for a presentation or performance;
- receive the same instructions;
- share perceptions about things that affect everyone;
- make a collective decision about things that affect everyone;
- develop the class's identity as a group.

Some of the reasons you can have for asking your pupils to work in small groups or teams include that you want them to have greater opportunities and responsibilities than they have in a whole-class format to:

- explore and contribute their ideas under their own steam;
- engage with their peers' ideas in detail or depth;
- have hands-on experience;
- control how they use time, space and resources;
- take specific roles, such as chairing or leading, posing questions, observing, making notes, summing up, reporting and so on;
- develop their cooperative, interpersonal and social skills and qualities;
- learn what advantages there can be in joint enterprise.

Reasons you can have for asking your pupils to work individually include that you want them to:

- work on their own agenda and their own choice of material, topic or skills;
- sustain concentration;
- formulate their own ideas, perhaps prior to sharing them with a group or the whole class;
- find out and/or show what they can do independently;
- focus on how their ideas compare with other people's ideas;
- develop their individual sense of control, responsibility and achievement.

How can you use questioning in your lessons?

Tests and examinations are a specific context in which your pupils have independently to answer questions and comply with instructions. The work your pupils do as a class and in groups and small teams can be seen in part as helping them learn how to address questions and tasks they are likely to meet when they are being assessed for the purpose of summing up what they know. You can try to make connections between questions your pupils are interested in and questions that are on your agenda and meet requirements they ultimately have to face.

In a traditional, didactic model of teaching and learning, a teacher or assistant has the knowledge; a teacher or assistant asks the questions; and a teacher or assistant verifies, corrects or gives pupils the answers. Didactic teaching risks producing superficial, short-term learning. For lasting, significant learning to take place, that dynamic has to change or be offset by other models.

When the agenda belongs to you and your assistants, authority for asking the questions and knowing 'right' answers lies with you. But when your pupils have a voice in the agenda, authority for asking questions can be shared by them, and coming up with answers can be open to everyone. In good lessons, authority and initiative flow to and fro between teachers, assistants and pupils.

If things go well, your pupils' interior dialogue with themselves is born of the conversations they have with other people, including one another and you. The habits they form in talking and listening with teachers and assistants, with one another and with themselves, can be vital to their development of constructive attitudes. In authentic dialogue, both parties ask and answer questions. Your pupils' learning is likely to be enriched when answers are something to be found or worked out, rather than something merely to be stated. How can you encourage this in your lessons?

It matters what kinds of question are asked in lessons and assessments, and how they are asked. We can make a distinction between *convergent* and *divergent* questioning. Convergent questions have a specific answer, often a statement of what is taken to be a fact. Divergent questions have many possible answers and can be speculative. Harry Torrance and John Pryor (1998) have written very usefully about this in detail and about its wider significance.

How much do you favour questioning that prompts short statements of supposed facts? How much do you favour questioning that promotes reasoning and imagination and accepts complexity and uncertainty? When is the time and what is the place for convergent thinking? And for divergent thinking? You can gain a great deal by discussing these matters with colleagues and by asking visitors to look out for the different kinds of question that are asked in your lessons. Still entirely relevant and helpful on this topic is the at-the-time groundbreaking book by Douglas Barnes, James Britton and Harold Rosen (*Language, the Learner and the School*, 1971).

When you ask convergent questions, you tend to:

- address the whole class;
- give your pupils cues and clues about what to think;
- expect prompt answers and press on with more questions at pace;
- control the line of thinking;
- know the answers and want your pupils to show they know them too;
- lead your pupils along a chain of facts or through a process of reasoning you want them to internalise;
- overlook which pupils are not with you, and so lose their attention and interest;
- avoid complex and open questions.

But it is possible to ask convergent questions in such a way that you:

- set different conditions or rules for answering on different occasions for different purposes: for example, giving time for reflection; requiring whole-sentence answers; randomly choosing who answers; hot-seating; asking your pupils to display their answers on boards or via a handheld digital device; having pupils answer in chorus;
- check the class' progress, for example, by having every pupil show her or his answer or by asking a 'hinge' question, which shows whether or not the class understands a key point; if they do not, you can adjust the pace, scope or direction of the teaching;
- use questions to inspire or structure an enquiry or project;
- do not know what the answer will be, because it is likely that only the person answering the question knows the answer;
- progress from relatively straightforward to more demanding questions over the course of a lesson or topic or unit.

When you ask divergent questions, you tend to:

- talk with a group or one-to-one, and, even when addressing the whole class, you show interest in what your pupils uniquely think;
- give room for alternative answers and lines of thinking;
- revise, open out or deepen the thinking;
- allow for uncertainty, doubt and not knowing;
- encourage awareness that people think differently and that even the same person can have different, yet viable answers to a question;
- expect your pupils to help decide where the thinking might go.

The answer to a convergent question judged to be correct implies, *That's it: the matter is closed.* An answer to a divergent question implies, *That's part of it: there's more to this.* This is not to suggest that convergent questioning has no value; sometimes it is good to have closure on a question. But it does not help your pupils if they are given the impression that closed answers to convergent questions guarantee understanding and capability.

Convergent questions, typically asked in quizzes, include many 'what', 'who', 'where' and 'when' questions, for example:

- *What are the names of shapes that have four sides?*
- *Which of these popular writers have you read?*

Convergent questions can also probe processes and matters that are vital to your pupils' learning in relation to significant areas, such as:

- *What did you do to work that out?*
- *What problem did these people face?*
- *Who thinks there's an easy solution here?*
- *When is knowing about ____ really useful?*

Examples of divergent questions, typical of relatively exploratory, open-ended enquiry, include many 'why', 'how', 'what if', speculative, procedural and conditional questions, for example:

- *How can you set out instructions?*
- *What would happen if ...?*
- *How can you work out what a decimal is in terms of a percentage?*
- *In what ways are you getting better at explaining your thinking?*
- *What advice would you give?*

Making relevant, coherent, precise responses to questions or instructions is a life skill. So too are entertaining alternative answers and tolerating ambiguity and ambivalence. Finite answers to relatively closed questions are an important part of formal tests and examinations. You and your colleagues can survey papers and rubrics to find out what kinds of question predominate and you can help one another find ways of planning lessons so that enough attention is given to preparing your pupils to meet the convergent demands that will be made of them, while still giving expression to their lateral, imaginative, creative thinking.

You and your colleagues can work on developing how questions are used in your lessons. You can do this by:

- examining different ways of setting up activities to stimulate fruitful thinking and questioning, for example, arranging seating so that pupils can see one another and so be more likely to listen to one another;
- analysing types of question that are used in parts of a lesson;
- sharing examples of productive questions and how to use them;
- collaborating in cross-curricular projects involving different kinds of questions and questioning;
- exploring questioning when you observe one another teach.

Questioning is enriched and made powerful when:

- your pupils, you and your assistants ask genuine questions you are interested in;
- questioners want to find out how, as well as what, respondents think;
- your pupils become aware of developing skills and qualities that help them ask and answer questions, such as thinking about the point of questions, not jumping to conclusions, and looking for alternative answers;
- your pupils grow to feel they are part of a community of learners, asking and tackling worthwhile questions.

How can you use computing to enrich your teaching and your pupils' learning?

The national curriculum in England is one example of how computing has evolved as an area of teaching and learning, defined from 2015 as comprising computer science, information technology and digital literacy.

What was previously thought of as information and communications technology (ICT) has become computational thinking and creativity with the aim of understanding and changing the world for the better. In one respect, computing is a subject in its own right, in the same way that science, mathematics, English and so on are subjects. In another respect, it is computational literacy, a strand in cross-curricular teaching and learning that is comparable to the literacies of speaking, listening, reading and writing, numeracy and emotional, personal and social literacies. So it makes sense for computing to be taught in both discrete and embedded ways, just as those other capabilities need to be.

How your school approaches computing may be a part of how it organises, makes and evaluates provision for cross-curricular aspects and areas of learning. You need to work with colleagues in your team and across your school to agree what your responsibilities are regarding your pupils' learning computer science, information technology and digital literacy. You want to know:

- What computing knowledge, skills and understanding are your pupils expected to develop in subjects you teach?
- What activities and resources do your pupils engage with in other teachers' lessons that may relate to the learning objectives you have as priorities, for example, data logging, computer-aided design, word processing, using online diagrams and images, using devices such as a remote mouse palette and so on?

- How might you capitalise on the expertise and interests in computing that your pupils have, so that everyone might benefit from what they know?

- How will you try to manage a balance between your pupils' being instructed in computing and their using computing independently?

- What balance will your pupils have between whole-class sessions, solo, paired and small-group working involving computing?

- What opportunities will your pupils have to use their computing skills to contribute to aspects of school life, for example, operating school radio and producing teaching materials, films, publications, media texts, promotional material and so on?

- What training, technical and teaching guidance and support are available to you for planning, teaching, assessing, recording and reporting your pupils' computing learning and achievements?

- What links can you and your colleagues have with other educators and organisations in order to share computing experience and expertise, for example, local and leading schools and internet sites for pioneers and practitioners such as FilmsforLearning (go to www.makewav.es/thomashardyeschool/c/filmsforlearning and *www.youtube.com/user/filmsforlearning*)?

Chris Watkins wrote a powerful two-sided pamphlet on contrasting uses of technology (2002), available via his website.

Summing up

- Your pupils' confidence in you as their teacher depends on the extent to which you care about their learning.

- The better you can diagnose underlying causes and factors in difficulties your pupils experience, the better you can prepare activities that help them develop dispositions and qualities of mind essential to deep learning. These include willingness to think about how they deal with uncertainty, misunderstanding and error.

- You want your pupils to be engaged in interesting and worthwhile activities for as much of their time as possible. Variations in their working as a whole class, as pairs and groups and individually can help them sustain their attention and interest.

- When your pupils have a voice in the agenda for their activities, authority for asking questions can pass to them, and coming up with answers can be open to anyone. In good lessons, authority flows to and fro between teachers, assistants and pupils.

References

Barnes, D., Britton, J. and Rosen, H. (1971) *Language, the Learner and the School.* Harmondsworth, UK: Penguin Books.

Blythe, R. (1969, 2005) *Akenfield: Portrait of an English Village.* London, UK: Penguin Books.

Bunting, M. (2016) 'Crisis in Care', *The Essay*, Episode 4, BBC Radio 3. www.bbc.co.uk/programmes/b04dwbkt/episodes/player.

Channel 4 Television, David Clews (2011) *Educating Essex*; David Brindleburn and Grace Reynolds (2013) *Educating Yorkshire*; David Clews (2014) *Educating the East End*; Nicola Brown and Alex Kohler (2015) *Educating Cardiff.* London, UK: Twofour.

FilmsforLearning (n.d.). www.makewav.es/thomashardyeschool/c/filmsforlearning; www.youtube.com/user/filmsforlearning.

Gawande, A. (2014) *Being Mortal: What Matters in the End.* London, UK: Profile Books.

Hannam, C., Smyth, P. and Stephenson, N. (1973) *Young Teachers and Reluctant Learners: The Story of the Hillview Project.* Harmondsworth, UK: Penguin papers in education, Penguin Books.

Lane, H. (1928) *Talks to Parents and Teachers.* London, UK: George Allen and Unwin.

Lemov, D. (2010) *Teach Like a Champion: 49 Techniques That Put Students on the Path to College.* San Francisco, CA: Jossey-Bass.

Marsh, H. (2014) *Do No Harm: Stories of Life, Death and Brain Surgery.* London, UK: Weidenfeld & Nicholson.

O'Connell, B. (1998, 2005) *Solution-Focused Therapy.* London, UK: Sage Publications.

Philibert, N. (2002) *Être et avoir.* France: Maia Films and Les Films d'ici.

Rogers, C. (1961, 1995) *On Becoming a Person: A Therapist's View of Psychotherapy.* New York: Houghton Mifflin Books.

Sacks, O. (2015) *On the Move: A Life.* London, UK: Picador.

Torrance, H. and Pryor, J. (1998) *Investigating Formative Assessment: Teaching, Learning and Assessment in the Classroom.* Buckingham: Open University Press.

Watkins, C. (2002) 'Today I visited a primary school that is becoming famous for its use of technology,' in N. Pachler (Ed.), *Lehren und Lernen mit IKT* (Informations- und Kommunikationstechnologie). Part 1. Innsbruck, Austria: Studienverlag.

Helping your pupils act and think, think and act

Alternating standing back with becoming immersed in activity plays a vital part in your pupils' developing self-awareness and autonomy. This chapter explores your pupils' self-assessment, peer assessment and engaging with other people's appraisals as crucial to their making good use of feedback, criteria and targets. An account will also be given of how useful it can be for your pupils to teach one another, learn from one another and think about what makes a good observer, a good teacher and a good learner.

What part does conscious effort play in your pupils' learning?

Your pupils' thinking and learning can be automatic and unconscious, particularly when they are playing, or when they are intent on what they are doing or involved in exploratory, creative activities they enjoy. When your pupils are fully engaged, they take for granted what they want to achieve and instinctively understand what standards they are aiming for and hence what criteria might be used to judge what they do.

Tacit concentration can be a good part of becoming competent or expert in an activity, and it is typical of spontaneous, voluntary learning. Teaching strategies can be designed to promote such learning, and the younger learners are, the more this applies. This kind of teaching works less by instructing learners and more by creating environments that stimulate and facilitate learners' involvement in and control over what they do. The younger learners are, the less likely they are to articulate goals and judgements in what they do. The more mature and more capable they are, the more they can pursue public, negotiable intentions and rewards.

Your pupils do not have to put their minds to everything they learn, but some learning depends on self-conscious effort and thinking. Important aspects of learning can be improved when learners plan, monitor and review what they do. This applies particularly to the kinds of learning that schools promote.

As their teacher, you are an advocate for your pupils. That is to say, you sometimes speak and act on their behalf and in their interests. Your advocacy underpins your decisions about what activities might benefit their wellbeing and learning. When you stimulate and facilitate their learning through playful, inventive activity, for example, you take responsibility for *what they are trying to do*, *what they are getting better at* and *what they might do to develop further*. Your advocacy wanes as their experience and awareness of autonomy and interdependence develop.

Your pupils are likely to focus deliberately on what they do when they:

- choose and design activities for themselves;
- try to teach others;
- look critically at what they do;
- are asked to do things they do not immediately find appealing or intriguing;
- lack relevant skills and understanding;
- get stuck or go wrong;
- are interrupted or put off.

When your pupils plan and reflect on their activity, they have a chance to focus on what they want to achieve and consciously consider standards they aim for and, hence, what criteria apply. This concentration can be a vital part of becoming competent or expert in an activity, especially if it is something they do not initially set out to learn for themselves.

How can you help your pupils learn by assessing themselves and one another?

The better your pupils take note of how well they reach and how far they fall short of standards they aim to achieve, the better their learning is likely to be.

As learners mature, they can benefit from teaching strategies designed to help them think about what they do: by assessing themselves, by assessing one another and by being assessed by you and other people. The younger they are, the more they do these things intuitively and implicitly, via body language, gesture and tone of voice. And even as adults, we continue to learn from many different forms of tacit as well as explicit self-criticisms and judgements by others.

D. Royce Sadler (1989) explained how self-assessment is an essential part of developing insight and competence. His analysis was that, for learners to get better at using complex skills and concepts, they have to check how well they are doing while they are doing it. This means they have to use target standards, inherent in good quality work, to inform their efforts. In this sense, learning entails pupils emulating or surpassing standards they are aware of as pertinent to their goals. It means that learners have to change what they do to bring it closer to what they aim for.

Sadler saw that teaching methods are inadequate if they do not enable learners to check their own progress towards the standards they aim to meet, consciously or otherwise. For learners to fulfil their potential, they need to develop attitudes and skills that support self-assessment in activities they feel they are in charge of. So you do well to ask your pupils to:

- study the manner of and reasons for other people's success and lack of success;
- study how successful their own and others' efforts are;
- focus on what they see they must do to achieve high standards;
- check how well they are doing while they are doing it;
- try to teach others.

The research suggests that it is far from easy or straightforward to fulfil these intentions in teaching, not least when you are made to feel anxious about 'delivering results'. You can be tempted, for the sake of speed or to placate authorities, to do too much for your pupils, but this prevents them from learning for themselves what they need to understand, do and remember. In his research summary, Sadler (2010) presented a critical view of teachers' fairly common practice of giving learners feedback on strengths and weaknesses in their work with suggestions for improvement. Though learners apparently appreciate it, Sadler showed that that kind of feedback has little or no impact on performance and learning, despite teachers' well-meaning intentions and the time and effort they put into it.

This is not an argument in favour of withholding information from your pupils about what they are expected to do, how they will be assessed and what they might focus on. Rather, the case is strongly made that they need to engage in activities that enable them, through experience, to construct for themselves the specific skills and understandings that are involved in the capabilities they are trying to develop.

Sadler's analysis was that your efforts are undermined if you behave as though 'telling, even detailed telling, is the most appropriate route to improvement in complex learning' (p. 548). Telling your pupils things is unlikely to enable them to make the necessary dynamic connections between the information available to them, the work they do and how they might develop further. For significant, adaptive learning to take place, your pupils require much more than being told what to do or rehearsed in performances they cannot command.

I discovered this in my fourth year of teaching. I was developing a practice of handing over chunks of time to my pupils to use on activities of their own design. Some of them would choose to work on their own; others would pair up or work as a group. Each of them had to decide what they wanted to achieve over a sequence of initially four lessons spanning a couple of weeks. At the start, they had to say what help they needed and how they wanted their efforts to be commented on and by whom. If they wanted to change their minds as they went along, we could talk about it. The class would get going, and I found I was able to do much more teaching in those lessons than I normally managed. They would come in and immediately get on with their work. I spent every second talking with individuals or small groups about things that mattered to them. At the end of one lesson with a class of 13–14-year-olds, I felt I wanted to say something to them all and looked round. I was too late; change-over time had come and everyone was leaving the room. I realised I had not spoken collectively to the class during the 70 minutes, not once. A teacher of art, design technology or computing or an early-years teacher might say, *How come it took you so long to work that out? We work like that all the time.* But for me it was a 'light-bulb moment': I knew, *That's what I'd like all my lessons to be like.* The main difference it made to my teaching was that my pupils asked me to talk to them about things I wanted to teach them. I did not have to cajole them or listen to their excuses. I had to help them to do what they had set their sights on. They decided what to do next and, if they didn't know, they would consult someone. They shared ideas amongst themselves and enjoyed what their classmates were achieving. They assessed themselves and one another and were interested in my assessments because they asked for them. Those lessons belonged to them.

How can you help your pupils develop self-awareness and conscious effort?

This is an example of how one teacher developed her teaching. With her class of 7–8-year-olds in Portsmouth, the United Kingdom (UK), she decided to emphasise key objectives for particular pieces of written work by outlining the success criteria to be used in assessing their efforts. Before the pupils handed in their work, they had to respond to questions, for example:

> *Task*: Writing a fable
> *Success Criteria*:
> *Does your fable have a character or characters which are animals?*
> *Have you described your main character/s?*
> *Have you described your setting?*
> *Has your fable got a beginning, a middle and an end?*
> *What is the moral of your fable?*
> *Was there anything that you found very difficult about this task? If so, what was it?*

As the class progressed, the teacher was keen to develop a more differentiated approach. She chose to refine the success criteria by using the words *must*, *should* and *could*.

> *Task*: Write a character portrait of someone you know or someone you imagine.
> *Success Criteria*:
> *You **must** write a portrait of a character.*
> *You **should** use some describing words.*
> *You **could** use some interesting or special adjectives or some similes, e.g. red as a cherry.*

June Hutchinson was working at the same time on the same project at Springfield School, Portsmouth, UK. This is how she described what she and her modern foreign languages colleagues were doing.

> *I think the biggest focus for development is thrusting the ownership back onto our pupils. In a way we hypercorrect every piece of work they do, and give them the answers. We go through and make the corrections, and I'm desperately trying to pull away from that and put the onus back onto them. So with written work I will underline and put question marks, but I won't correct. And asking them, 'Well, what is the problem then? Why have I done that?' and so in assessment for learning we're moving away from giving them A, B, Cs or a number.*
>
> *It's got to the point where pupils will write, 'This is really scruffy,' which makes me chuckle because it's so much better coming from them than from me, so I just write, 'I agree' ... . Having gone through and done the underlinings, and question marks and the little arrows, I give them their work back and they have then got time – and this is the really crucial bit – to put it right. In the past we have not ever done that; we've tended to give a book back, it's got a grade B, 'Right, turn to the next clean page and let's get on with today's work'.*
>
> *We have got to slow down. If we are wanting them to improve the quality of their speaking and their writing, we've got to pay it more attention. It is no good leaving out that final step because we will never see a difference if our pupils don't look at their*

Continued

> *comments and make a correction, or ask for help if they're stuck or put right spellings and write them out. The whole system will fall down if we don't do that final stage.*

The teachers involved in these developments reflected Sadler's research (see Blanchard, 2009). In Sadler's view, the most effective teaching includes making 'intensive use of purposeful peer assessment as a pedagogical strategy, not just for assessment but also for teaching the substantive content of the course' (2010, p. 548). Peer assessment is, in some ways, an extension of self-assessment. It enables learners to use their own vernaculars to communicate in pertinent detail about what they are aiming to achieve and how to judge and improve their efforts. Those who 'get' the lesson or topic can mediate its concepts, terminology and methods for their peers and, in doing so, reinforce and/or revise their own understanding. They can help one another focus on instructions, examples of good work, assessment criteria and personal targets.

Assessing one another's work, your pupils can press on one another's weak intentions. Without a sufficient will to succeed, their learning may remain shallow and short-lived. Your challenge is to be alert to how well your pupils work together in their twos and threes. If they collude with one another in taking easy routes, you need to rejig the groupings or show them good examples of mutual coaching that bring the best out of them.

This is an example of peer-assessment. Learners tackle a task as individuals, and then, as a pair or where necessary a three, they:

- Remind themselves of what they have been trying to do by:
  - checking their instructions
  - checking their targets or criteria
  - telling one another what makes the examples of work they have looked at successful
- Take turns to study their efforts and ask themselves what shows they have reached a good standard, and what would need to be changed to make their work even better.

Assessment by observers and critics can enhance their self-assessment and peer assessment. These are all versions of formative assessment, as explained by Paul Black and Dylan Wiliam (1998), who used the idea of a 'gap', proposed by Arkalgud Ramaprasad (1983), that learners:

- see the difference between what they want to achieve and their present ability to achieve it;
- try to close the gap in an effort to reach their goal;
- decide how well they have done;
- consider ways of continuing to learn.

Crucial in this, therefore, are learners' volition and agency.

Here is an example of a strategy, explained to me by Steve Parker, about an aspect of his teaching in Northamptonshire, UK, which blends all of the themes discussed so far. Wanting to make his marking manageable and effective, he would choose a significant part of a pupil's writing or digital file to comment on in detail, and the pupil would have to act on the prompts and questions he gave them. He would tell the class that he wanted them to get maximum value out of concentrating on one paragraph or section of their work. Sometimes he would ask them to indicate which section they wanted him to pay special attention to. Once they were accustomed to it, Parker asked his pupils to use this routine in pairs to peer-mark one another's work. Before they handed their work over to their partner, they could highlight a paragraph or section they wanted to have feedback on. Then they marked each other's work and followed up the guidance they received.

In these ways, your pupils' assessing one another can merge into their setting targets for one another and teaching one another.

How can you help your pupils learn by using targets?

Targets can also be called *personal* or *individual goals, aims, intentions, objectives, purposes* or *aspirations* for learning. Lesson objectives and individual pupils' targets differ in several ways.

Targets can be a natural extension of formative assessment, turning criteria, by which you and your pupils can judge performance, into qualities, skills and knowledge to work on. Targets can express personal standards your pupils set for themselves and/or public standards they recognise as relevant to their needs and goals. They are as useful as the conversations they generate and tend to be most successful when your pupils refer to them spontaneously as part of what they are doing.

For my book *Teaching and Targets: Self-Evaluation and School Improvement* (Blanchard, 2002) I visited nine rural, town and conurbation schools (one first, three primary, one middle, three secondary and one special) in four southern English local authorities. I wanted to learn about what using targets

Lesson objectives...	Pupils' targets...
are usually set by you or are taken over by you from authoritative or commercial schemes	may be set by you or by the pupil or may be devised jointly
may be for a whole class or you may differentiate them for groupings within a class	are usually for individual pupils and can reflect their personal aspirations
usually last for a lesson but may extend over a sequence of lessons	may last until they are hit or for as long as they continue to motivate and guide your pupils
tell the class what you want to achieve or what you want them to achieve	state what aspects of performance or learning an individual pupil will try to develop
can help your pupils be clear about what to do and how to go about it	state what your pupils are aiming for and give them insight into what they are getting better at
are usually referred to by you as a check on progress	need chiefly to be referred to by individual pupils to check their own and sometimes one another's progress
may be recorded to satisfy managers' or inspectors' requirements	may be recorded to inform your ongoing conversations with individual pupils; may also be recorded to support individual pupils' education planning and provision
can be used to gauge what has been achieved in terms of what you set out to do	help focus feedforward and feedback for individual pupils
can be modified in the light of experience for possible future use	serve as a focus of attention for as long as they remain valid and may inform records of progress and choices of work to be included in individual pupils' portfolios

can mean to pupils and teachers. The pupils I met said they saw targets as benefiting their motivation and achievement inasmuch as targets contributed to their sense of one or more of the following:

- what they were doing;
- why they were doing it;
- how they were setting about what they did;
- what they were good at and getting better at;
- what they might try to do to develop further.

Not one of my sample of nearly 600 5–18-year-old pupils indicated that using targets had transformed their school or classroom experience. None seemed to think having targets guaranteed good teaching or successful learning. They found little positive meaning in targets when they felt they were used merely because they had to be used. Generally, they took targets for granted as belonging to what they expected of school routines. Most of the pupils I interviewed and spoke to in discussion groups said targets were 'quite useful', and a minority were confident that their targets added positively to their motivation, focus and success. At worst, they thought targets made little difference to how well they did. More positively, a significant minority of pupils said having targets helped them know what their strengths were and how to improve their efforts. A good number of pupils said that their targets helped them to work well with their teachers, with one another and with adults other than teachers, so for them the social and collaborative benefits seemed to count most. In such cases, it seemed, using targets was linked in the pupils' minds with their experiences of one-to-one reviews, mentoring or other kinds of attention to their ongoing teaching and learning.

A number of schools had introduced target-setting schemes that collapsed because the processes meant little either to the teachers or to the pupils. Some schools continued target setting only to 'tick a box' and thereby placate inspectors or other authorities. Here are some points to bear in mind arising from that research.

About using targets

- When they work, targets focus your pupils' effort. They give direction to the steps your pupils take, so they are best expressed in terms of what your pupils intend to do and achieve.

- Your pupils might have targets of different kinds and durations. Their targets might have to do with social or behavioural aspects of what they do. They might have to do with key concepts or skills. They might last for a lesson or two or for the duration of a topic or unit of work. The younger pupils are, the more their targets need to be built into the way their activities are set up and carried out and the shorter-term their targets need to be.

- It makes sense, when you and your pupils use targets, to avoid trivial aspects of your pupils' performance and concentrate on what can make a significant difference to their learning.

- Having a target guarantees nothing. Having set a target, your pupils need to decide how to go about trying to achieve it: what steps will they take; what support might they want?

- Having hit a target, your pupils can express what they have learnt and learnt to do.

- When it is helpful, targets and follow-up comments can be noted as they emerge in discussion. On a cautionary note, sometimes using targets has failed because paperwork, storing data and administration have mattered more than pupils' learning.

- It is useful for you and your pupils to reflect on what you and they learn by using targets.

These are examples of practices that some schools have evolved through much trial and error.

How we help our pupils know what to aim for

Periodically, each class teacher or tutor has a one-to-one meeting with each pupil to discuss successes and areas for improvement, leading to a choice of no more than three goals.

At some stage in every topic or unit, we try to make sure every pupil is aware of a personal focus of attention in addition to overall learning objectives for the class.

Pupils sometimes have cards or a place in their book or folder to record their goals, with a date and a space for comments on progress and achievement.

Pupils who have individual education plans to meet their special needs may be used to trying to be precise about what to work on and how to check their progress. Their experience has made clear the value of individual pupils' expressing what they aim for in their own words. Here are examples of pupils' targets and the kinds of awareness and decisions they can lead to.

Targets chosen by three pupils			
	I am going to work on explaining my working.	*I want to be accurate when I take measurements.*	*My thing to work on now is reading every day.*
What the pupils decided			
So I need to …	*… take my time because it's not easy.* *… take each step and say what I did.*	*… check three times I have got the right numbers.* *… compare what I do with someone else.*	*… ask people to recommend writers to me.* *… have a good place to read in.*
And subsequently reflected			
Now I can …	*… go back over my thinking and see what I did right and where I went wrong.* *… say things with maths words, like subtraction means take away.*	*… measure lengths and weights.* *… see if my estimate turns out right.*	*… enjoy stories and some factual books.* *… find books I like to read.*

Thinking about this now I see ...	... you can check where you went wrong. But you have to make yourself do it. ... sometimes you have to ask if you are using the right method. ... there are different ways of solving problems.	...I am taking more care with my work. ... I was sometimes letting my team down. ... proper measuring really matters.	... I have to make myself read because I find it hard. ... I like reading on my own, but have to remember to do it. ... I have found some really good writers I didn't know before, like ....

One way of helping your pupils think about what they aim for is to give them examples. You might offer them a selection of cards, an interactive whiteboard screen of possibilities or a display board of options. Your suggestions might relate to generic aspects of learning or to a topic your pupils have begun or are going to work on. Here are some illustrations of what your pupils concentrate on.

Examples of what your pupils can focus on

- Preparing well and being organised;
- benefiting from other people's ideas;
- considering different ways of doing things;
- checking and improving first efforts;
- practising and being precise.

How can you help your pupils learn by teaching one another?

Pupils' teaching one another belongs to their cooperating and in some ways is an extension of their assessing one another. Taking a teaching role formalises your pupils' passing on what they know to one another.

Stuart Hampshire (1989) explained the vital part played in the growth of self-awareness and autonomy when we alternate standing back with becoming immersed:

> We could not ever be observers unless we were sometimes active experimenters, and we could not ever be experimenters unless we were sometimes observers. To observe is to learn what obstructions, instructions and constructions there are in the environment; and to experiment is to act with a view to perceiving what happens when we act in a certain way.

(p. 53)

83

> *it is through the various degrees of self-consciousness in action, through more and more clear and explicit knowledge of what I am doing, that in the first place I become comparatively free.*
>
> (p. 174)

One of the most significant things you can do to engage your pupils' deeper learning is to enable them to observe one another while they are being taught. By teaching and observing one other, your pupils can see what makes it difficult and what makes it easy for their peers to learn. M. L. (Jane) Johnson Abercrombie (1960) came to understand this through her experiments designed to find how best to enable students of medicine, architecture and education to sharpen and deepen their thinking. In one case, her teaching objective was for medical students to learn to make diagnostic use of radiology plates. The same could apply to teaching anyone to interpret what they see, hear and so on. It became clear that her students were not able to read an X-ray as if it spoke to them, nor did it help them to be told what to see. Images, like texts, need interpretation, and interpretation is something individuals have constructively and creatively to do for themselves, albeit and most usefully working with other people (see Lev Vygotsky, 1962, 1986, 2012). Abercrombie's insight was that 'How to tell students what to look for without telling them what to see is the dilemma of teaching' (1960, p. 63).

Abercrombie created conditions, via a strategy she called *free* or *associative discussion*, enabling her students to explore their own and one another's thinking. Her focus was on creating conditions for them to reassess and rearrange what they already 'knew' rather than receive 'new packets of facts'. This involved her students' saying what they saw and comparing that with what their peers said. They were helped to discriminate between facts and opinions, resist false conclusions and address problems they encountered. It emerged that focused, mutually supportive discussion brought a more effective range of factors into play than could be achieved by didactic teaching.

So the solution she found to her teaching dilemma and to the problem of her students' learning was to enable them to compare and contrast one another's ideas. She enabled them to tolerate diversity of views, ambiguity and their own uncertainties and so learn to be collaborative and rigorous in critically examining their own and one another's interpretations.

You can plan for this kind of teaching in your lessons. You can ask your pupils to work in twos and threes and larger groups, to express their own ideas and to pay close attention to what everyone says. They can become used to asking: *Why should we think this rather than that? What did we first think? What do we think now? What has changed our minds? What do we still not know? How could we take this further?*

This kind of learning is promoted by a programme that was developed by the Society for the Advancement of Philosophical Enquiry and Reflection in Education (SAPERE), funded by the Education Endowment Foundation and evaluated by Stephen Gorard *et al.* (2015) at Durham University in the UK. Success depends on the programme's becoming a regular part of the weekly timetable. The focus was on helping 8–10-year-old pupils become more willing and able to learn from one another by asking questions and making reasoned arguments. The evaluation concluded that concentrating on those skills had a positive impact on their attainment, with pupils making approximately two months' additional progress in reading and mathematics during the course of a year. Learning to think and discuss also noticeably helped pupils' confidence in speaking and listening. And socially disadvantaged pupils made the biggest gains.

Building on these insights, you can give your pupils practice in working as threes or small teams, rotating roles of teaching, learning and observing. They might focus on anything relating to their current learning and use any media and materials that help, including, for example, YouTube clips, if you have sufficient portable computers. You can explain how each of them has to take each role in turn.

Be a better learner by teaching and observing one another

- *When you are being the **teacher**, you have to show or explain to a partner how to do something and help her or him without doing it for her or him.*
- *When you are being the **learner**, you have to pay attention, ask questions and try to do what you are being taught.*
- *When you are being the **observer**, you have to look and listen out for what the teacher does that helps the learner and for what the learner does that helps her or him learn.*

At the end of the teaching and learning episode, the observer sums up what she or he has noticed about what helps the teaching and learning go well. All three finish by deciding and then sharing with the whole class:

- *What makes a good observer?*
- *What makes a good teacher?*
- *What makes a good learner?*

Your pupils' understanding and capability develop with their increasing confidence and skill in the three roles.

To support your development as teachers, you and your colleagues can use the same activity. You might focus, for example, on modelling, questioning, explanation, responsiveness, vocabulary, sentence length or whatever you and your colleagues want to work on.

Summing up

- To learn well, your pupils need to engage in activities that enable them through experience to construct for themselves the specific skills and understandings that are involved in the capabilities they are trying to develop.

- By assessing themselves and one another, your pupils can learn to bring what they do closer to what they aim for.

- Targets turn criteria, by which you and your pupils can judge their performance, into qualities, skills and knowledge to work on developing. Targets are as useful as the conversations they generate, and tend to be most successful when your pupils refer to them spontaneously as part of what they are doing.

- When your pupils discuss and work together in healthy, constructive ways, they are teaching one another, albeit informally.

- Your pupils can learn a great deal by teaching one another, observing teaching, and deciding what makes a good observer, a good teacher, and a good learner. The same applies to you and your colleagues.

References

Black, P. and Wiliam, D. (1998) 'Assessment and classroom learning', *Assessment In Education*, 5, 1:7–74.

Blanchard, J. (2002) *Teaching and Targets: Self-Evaluation and School Improvement.* London, UK: Routledge/Falmer.

Blanchard, J. (2009) *Teaching, Learning and Assessment.* Maidenhead, UK: Open University Press.

Gorard, S., Siddiqui, N. and See, B. H. (2015) *Philosophy for Children: Evaluation Report and Executive Summary.* Durham, UK: Durham University.

Hampshire, S. (1989) *Thought and Action.* London, UK: Chatto & Windus.

M. L. Johnson Abercrombie (1960) *The Anatomy of Judgement: An Investigation into the Processes of Perception and Reasoning.* London, UK: Hutchinson.

Ramaprasad, A. (1983) 'On the definition of feedback', *Behavioural Science*, 28, 4–13.

Sadler, D. R. (1989) 'Formative assessment and the design of instructional systems', *Instructional Science*, 18, 119–144.

Sadler, D. R. (2010) 'Beyond feedback: developing student capability in complex appraisal', *Assessment & Evaluation in Higher Education*, 35, 5: 535–550.

Vygotsky, L. (edited and with a foreword by Alex Kozulin) (1962, 1986, 2012) *Thought and Language.* Cambridge, MA: The MIT Press.

Planning to frame your pupils' thinking

This chapter discusses the roles that perceiving and using patterns play in your pupils' cognitive development. We will analyse how shaping their thinking can enable them to meet the demands that school makes of them. We will explore how you can make schemas an explicit focus of your pupils' attention and study and thereby help them think for themselves. Examples of schemas are presented across a range of curriculum areas and across a range of age groups. Finally, a framework for planning sequences of lessons is presented.

What are schemas, and why are they important in children's cognitive development?

You can feel under pressure to 'cover the curriculum' and teach too much too quickly. To resist moving on too soon, you need confidence, and other people's seeing it as your responsibility, to adapt your teaching to what you see your pupils need.

Your teaching cannot give your pupils their learning as though it were a drink or a present. How well they learn is tied up with how hard they try. And how well your pupils direct their efforts depends on how they frame intentions, choose processes and see results, all served by their using what they know. Memory, both conscious and unconscious, is at the heart of your pupils' developing competence and expertise. When your pupils say or show, *I've forgotten what we're doing (What am I meant to be doing?)*, or, *I don't know what it's meant to look like (Have I done it right?)*, you can try to help them remember or find out. When they say, *I know it, but I just can't think of it*, you can respond with, *What could remind you?* Or, *Shall we ask ___, who seems to have a way of remembering?* It is better not to remember for your pupils but to help them remember and learn for themselves.

Frederic Bartlett (1932) illustrated the role of memory in perception and performance using the example of hitting a ball. He explained that, as you move to hit the ball, you merge the sense you have of your intent with your awareness of your posture. Bartlett noted that how you position yourself is 'a result of a whole series of earlier movements, in which the last movement before the stroke has a predominant function', and, as you begin the action of striking the ball, you do not 'produce something absolutely new', nor do you ever 'merely repeat something old' (pp. 201–202).

We act and learn, learn and act, by constructing and reconstructing neural patterns, making and remaking mental and muscular maps. It might be tempting to think of these as blueprints, but schemas are never fixed in our brains. They are neither stored nor retrieved as film-loops, sound-tracks or data bytes. It is an ongoing part of our mental activity that we continually find similarities and differences, rules and exceptions in the world and in ourselves. This is schematic thinking, and it evolves with every iteration (see Chris Frith, 2007).

There is built-in decline and entropy as well as obsolescence in our learning. Nothing we learn is forever. More importantly, whenever we use what we have learned we remake it and so are in a position to learn something new. We might like to think we have 'got' knowledge or skill, which is fixed and stable and just has to be brought out of safe storage when we need it. But that is not how our brains work. It can be useful for your pupils to realise this: learning is all about making connections and realising patterns, time and again, but without duplicating what went before. We might improve our capacity to learn by understanding that we have to construct knowledge and skill for ourselves actively and creatively through and for each moment of our experience. If we think there is an easier option of just swallowing knowledge or imbibing skill, we are unlikely to commit sufficiently to our experience and what it can teach us.

If to learn is to develop schemas, then to teach is to stimulate and facilitate learners' practical, schematic thinking. Jean Piaget (1952) was among the first to research the part played by schemas in learning and development, charting how children are prompted by their biological maturation and environmental experience to progressively reorganise their mental processes. He found that children develop cognitively, first by constructing their understanding of themselves and things around them, and second by responding positively to discrepancies between what they understand and how they are made to think again.

Chris Athey (1990, 2007) studied how infants use retraceable thoughts and actions to assimilate and accommodate what they realise. For example, 'gazing' is a part of learning how things are positioned and 'tracking' a part of learning how things move. Infants take things in and out of containing spaces, wrap things up, cover and uncover things, implicitly yet purposefully finding ways to control themselves and their environment.

Birch Farm in Suffolk, the United Kingdom (UK), is an example of a nursery that builds on Athey's work and arranges activities for young children based on observations of their behaviours and interests (see www.birchfarm.co.uk/schemas.htm). It shows how teaching can engage with children's inherent and emerging cognitive structures and initiatives. Here are my versions of two of their examples.

Schema	Activities	Extension ideas
Orientation: trying different points of view, physically as well as figuratively	Turn things over; look behind pictures and other objects	Take different stances, for example, viewing from above and below, right way up and upside down, from close up and far away … Say what different characters saw/felt, for example, Goldilocks and Baby Bear
Connection and separation: seeing how things join and come apart	Build and dismantle; tie and untie knots	Make trains and carriages; use a stapler and other office materials to join paper and other things together; use linking devices such as Stickle bricks, Meccano, Lego …

Elizabeth Carruthers and Maulfry Worthington (2006) described how valuable it is to engage with children's cognitive instincts and inventions, in particular when they use objects, pictures and diagrams to help them count and make sense of numbers. Gordon Wells (1986) illuminated how crucial children's constructing and reconstructing stories are to their meaning-making. In *Closely Observed Children: The Diary of a Primary Classroom* by Michael Armstrong (1980) and in *The Enquiring Classroom: An Introduction to Children's Learning* by Stephen Rowland (1984), the authors made fascinating studies of their pupils' schematic learning across different subject areas.

How can using schematic thinking help your pupils respond to what school asks of them?

Jerome Bruner's research (1966) led him to see a teacher's role as enabling pupils to devise and infer principles. His view was that in teaching, you have vital decisions to make and act on, concerning:

- how ready your pupils are to engage in lesson activities;
- how you might combine illuminating models of thinking with thought-provoking activities;
- how you might sequence the schemas and activities you think will be helpful;
- how best to respond to your pupils' efforts.

That makes a powerful overall brief for your planning.

Our everyday thinking tends to be quick and unreflective (e.g. see Vilayanur Ramachandran, 2011; and Daniel Kahneman, 2011). School learning demands slower, more deliberate mental work, articulation and development. As you enable your pupils to try thinking more accurately and more potently than they mundanely need or care to, you offer them ways of thinking that have evolved through social innovation, technological development, scientific discovery and personal insight. And in return, as it were, your pupils may offer you schemas they use that you may not have met before.

To achieve academic validity and earn merit, your pupils' thinking has to be more disciplined and more overt than is their informal custom. That is why studying is more demanding than sounding off or having a chat or doing what you feel like. Margaret Donaldson explained an aspect of this in her excellent book *Children's Minds* (1978):

> [T]he normal child comes to school with well-established skills as a thinker. But his [or her] thinking is directed outwards on to the real, meaningful, shifting, distracting world. What is going to be required for success in our educational system is that he [or she] should learn to turn language and thought in upon themselves. He [or she] must become able to direct his [or her] own thought process in a thoughtful manner. … His [or her] conceptual system must expand in the direction of increasing ability to represent itself.
>
> (pp. 88–90)

School makes specific demands on your pupils' motivation and articulacy through its valuing of transparent modes of thinking. The learning your pupils do in relation to how they organise their thinking has greater power and is more lasting than the factual content they take on board. Your profoundest and furthest reaching contribution can be to your pupils' developing curiosity, creativity and criticality, all deriving from their enjoyment and empowerment in schematic thinking. So it is by prioritising schematic thinking in line with your teaching objectives that you can try to resist pressure to hasten from topic to topic. James Hobson at Springfield School, Portsmouth, UK said to me once that the most important skill he had developed was deciding what to leave out.

The cognitive freight of a schema has to find expression in a particular structure, register, genre and so on. As Marshall McLuhan (1964) declared, the medium is the message. An infant's gazing is what she or he takes in: she or he does not gaze abstractly or universally, but gazes at something, making her or his own sense of it on each occasion.

Examples of schemas

An arrangement of items one after another, giving information a characteristic shape, feel and function, a list is an example of a schema. The first time a child recognises what a list is, and perhaps the second, third and fourth time too and intermittently thereafter, she or he registers what is itemised and, at the same time, takes in, consciously or unconsciously, how the items are presented: not as a headline, sentence, question, hypothesis, poem or any other format, but as a list. Later, that understanding is taken for granted as the list/schema is absorbed into automatic perception and behaviour. When she or he knows *this is a list* and *this is what listing things can do for us*, her or his mind has a specific power. That is how significant schemas are.

Schema	Functions
Listing	Naming and collecting things that are seen to belong together; itemising components
Sequencing	Showing order or chronology, stating *first, second ..., in the beginning, once, then, next, finally, in conclusion, ever after* ...
Comparing and contrasting	Describing similarities and differences between things; identifying advantages and disadvantages, strengths and weaknesses and so on
Representing	Using metaphors, codes, symbols and analogies to make one thing stand for another; understanding differences between literalness and figurativeness
Making variations	Changing one or more feature; adding, subtracting and transforming
Realising different ways of proceeding	Weighing up alternatives, for example, recognising varied ways of expressing the same thing, such as using synonyms and paraphrasing; considering methodologies for design and production, enquiry and experiment
Giving a definition	Identifying distinctive features; deciding what to include and what to exclude
Making a fair test	Testing a hypothesis; experimentally defining, following, evaluating and revising procedures
Delineating sets and categories	Grouping and classifying things that have qualities in common, for example, as Venn diagrams
Explaining causes and effects	Tracing how things come about; identifying origins and consequences and the foundations, conditions or precursors required for or conducive to something
Constructing models	Showing arrangements and how processes, mechanisms and systems work
Recognising relationships	Showing connection, association, affiliation, superordination, subordination and so on between and amongst things, for example, by means of spider- and flow-diagrams, hierarchies and taxonomies
Recognising equivalence and equality	Showing things with the same value, for example, in equations

Continued

Using criteria	Defining, applying and revising reference points to make judgements
Testing a rule, law or proposition	Analysing the grounds for stating what might be right or true
Using evidence and reasoning	Identifying strengths and weaknesses in propositions

You and your pupils do not have to wait to realise accidentally and unconsciously how they can organise their thinking to help them understand and invent. You can bring schemas into focus for them through their activities.

Your pupils may learn more effectively when you are conscious of helping them realise how useful it can be to make lists, sequences, comparisons, categories, representations, changes, definitions and so on for the purposes of finding things out, telling stories, persuading and so on.

What can schemas look like in the contexts of different curriculum areas?

Here are some examples for pupils of different ages in a range of curriculum areas.

Schemas across the curriculum and age range

Learning objective – To develop and perform your role in a dance ensemble.
Context and activity – Making a dance inspired by *The Lion King*.
Schema – We can make choices in our dancing according to:

□ Shape and character   □ Height and breadth
□ Pathway   □ Speed

(i) Shape your body to represent something or take on a character, for example, choosing which animal to imitate or 'become'. (ii) Position your body high or low, wide or narrow, for example, stretching, shrinking, leaping, crawling. (iii) Choose what directions to take in the available space and in relation to other dancers. (iv) Choose how fast to move, how to vary your pace and when to be still. These are concepts in action: ways of using our body and mind, giving an agenda for many lessons.
Learning objective – To practise how to keep a pulse when playing a tune.

Context and activity – Working towards being a marching band, for example, by developing confidence and concentration to play solo for peers to listen to; assessing one another's performances; and helping everyone develop.

Schema – We can learn to keep musical time by:

☐ Making physical movements   ☐ Observing others perform
☐ Following a conductor's beat   ☐ Performing for others

(i) Keep a beat in different ways, for example, tap a stick in time to music, move your hand in time, march to a tune. (ii) Watch and listen to someone else play music and think about how they keep time. (iii) Take your lead from a conductor's hand or baton. (iv) Perform for others in your class, in your school and other special audiences. This gives us ways of developing a skill that some of us instinctively find easier than others. It involves cycles and repetitions of listening, watching and doing, until these become virtually simultaneous and even automatic.

Learning objectives – To learn how to tackle two kinds of mathematical problem: 'change' and 'compare' problems.
Context and activity – Doing addition and subtraction, for example, using different ways of counting 'up' and 'down', such as physical objects and symbols to represent 'one', 'two' and so on; a number line.

Schema –   ☐ Making a numerical change to something
                      ☐ Seeing the numerical difference between things

Changing something can mean changing its value by adding or subtracting an amount, for example, 'Give this child two more toys, so how many has she now?' and, 'If you make this group smaller by three, how many will be left?' Comparing two or more things can mean describing how much more or less one is or has than another, for example, 'How much bigger is this than that?' 'Who is the tallest of the three?' 'How much faster are these than those?' This thinking helps your pupils see mathematics in living contexts and makes calculations much more than abstract, symbolic operations.

Learning objective – To construct a simple wind turbine capable of lifting weights.
Context and activity – Designing and making a three-bladed wind turbine, given a fixed base, to lift the greatest possible load at least 50 centimetres.
Schema – We can research, select and trial:

☐ Materials   ☐ Shapes   ☐ Sizes – length, width and thickness of blades

This thinking focuses on variables in problem solving: (i) investigating different materials, (ii) trialling different shapes, (iii) testing sizes and thicknesses of blades. This helps us develop skills and understanding in creative thinking, sharing ideas, controlling variables, being systematic, observing, recording findings and so on.
Learning objectives – To understand and remember French words.

Context and activity – Learning to say, listen to, read and write French.

Schema – □ Many English and French words have the same roots and patterns
□ Splitting words into syllables can show their meaning and give clues about how they are written

(i) You can try to spot words or bits of the words in French that sound and look like English. English has absorbed many Norman and borrowed many French words and expressions (*beef/boeuf, village/village, demander, parler…; bonbon, à la mode, savoir faire…*); French borrows from English (*un camping, week-end, un brainstorming…*); and English and French have Greek and Latin roots in common (*la géographie, l'histoire, les mathématiques, les sciences…; la télévision, la météo, l'enfant, en retard, le pneu…*). (ii) When you learn one word, you can access families of words. Seeing the sense of a particle or syllable in one word illuminates similar and related words; for example, *la géographie* is 'writing about the lands on this planet' because *géo-* means the Earth and *-graph-* means writing, and those elements appear in many other words; *cour-* in French means 'run', giving *courier, current, course, curriculum* and so on in English. We can spell words by breaking them into their parts: a syllable is a beat. If you close your lips and say *manger, dormir, porter*, you can hear the two beats making two syllables in each of those words and recognise the sense of *mange-, dorm-* and *port-*, linking to other words meaning 'eat', 'sleep' and 'carry'.
Learning objective – To prepare healthy, tasty food hygienically.

Context and activity – Baking scones and learning to look after yourself.

Schema – □ Cleanliness
□ Ingredients, appearance and texture
□ Sufficient cooking and tastiness

To prepare healthy food hygienically, it is important to make sure (i) hands, surfaces, equipment and so on are clean, (ii) the mixture has the right ingredients and the right look and texture, (iii) the food is well cooked and tasty. What is being taught here are some principles that underlie cooking generally. A focus can be on developing independent decision-making.

Learning objective – To describe a religion and its followers.
Context and activity – Studying religions.

Schema – □ View of 'God' □ Holy book
□ Rules for life □ Place and manner of assembly and rituals

We can use these concepts to discuss a religion: (i) how a religion constructs its deity/deities; (ii) what its written authority is; (iii) what its followers are instructed to do;

(iv) where and how they worship. This can point to what religions have in common as well as to what makes each of them unique.

Learning objective – To make a picture to represent what you see in greater depth than a simple line drawing.
Context and activity – Using Johannes Vermeer as a guide to making a drawing or painting of indoor or outdoor scenes.
Schema –   □ Perspective and proportion   □ Light and shade
Show relative distance from the viewer, comparative size of things and effects of light and shade. A range of techniques can be tried; for example, lines can be drawn to guide the marking out of objects in three-dimensional space and studies can be made of single objects to define light and shade.

Learning objective – To analyse characters in a story and explain why you think as you do.
Context and activity – Discussing John Steinbeck's novel *Of Mice and Men*.
Schema – Use pairs of contrasting qualities to highlight and explain differences between characters who:

□ are dreamers   □ see things as they are
□ act kindly   □ act unkindly

We can learn things about the craft of writing by studying how a novelist portrays characters in terms of their appearance, personalities and behaviour and how their lives turn out.

Learning objective – To evaluate the use of computer-assisted communications.
Context and activity – Solo or paired work designing advertising material for a fundraising event, using PowerPoint presentation software, spreadsheet models and web-pages.

Schema –   □ How well communication addresses its target audience
                      □ How fit for purpose communication is

Use specific criteria to judge how well computing helps achieve specific communication and business objectives. This gives hands-on experience, making and critiquing publicity material.

Learning objective – To prepare a comparative case study of earthquakes in two countries.

Context and activity – Understanding tectonic theory.

Schema – To analyse the aftermath of a geographical event, explain:

- ☐ The level of development in the locality and region
- ☐ The impact of the physical event on natural and built environments
- ☐ Consequences for social, economic and infrastructural aspects of people's lives

This focuses on interconnections between socio-economic factors and physical features such as terrain, the built environment and the effectiveness of services and organisations. Three linked dynamics can be studied: what causes earthquakes; what happens when an earthquake occurs; and how communities are affected.

Learning objective – To separate 'fact' from opinion in relation to specific historical events.

Context and activity – Evaluating evidence about processes of political, social and cultural change, in this case answering the question: 'Was life better under communism than in czarist Russia?'

Schema –
- ☐ Things that were gained and lost in social, political upheaval
- ☐ Freedoms that were affected by significant events, for example, religious worship, access to information, and participation in decision-making about public affairs

This prompts evidence-sifting and critical enquiry in order to 'triangulate' sources and analyse events. Consideration can be given to the validity of, for example, first-hand testimony, official reporting and historians' accounts.

Learning objectives – To receive and pass the basketball.

Context and activity – Playing basketball and learning to train in a sport.

Schema –
☐ Posture and movement	☐ Ball control
☐ Awareness of space and other players	☐ Tactics and decision-making

Focus on skill areas prior to applying them in competitive play, for example, (i) staying on your toes, bending your knees, swaying and so on; (ii) watching the ball, bouncing the ball with your fingers rather than your hand, changing hands and so on; (iii) looking up and around; (iv) feinting, switching direction, passing and so on. Practising and coaching can be done in different ways: solo, with partner and in a mini-game.

Learning objectives –To have a way of making ethical decisions about how to apply scientific knowledge.
Context and activity – Knowing how embryonic stem cells can be used to produce new tissues and deciding whether it is ethical to do so.

Schema –
- ☐ Respect for people's rights and duties
- ☐ Wanting decisions to be both rational and autonomous
- ☐ Wanting as far as possible to promote health and prevent or mitigate disease and so avoid harming people and/or the environment

This illustrates how explicit values can be used to guide decision-making in the applications of science. There is a focus here on (i) the legal and moral contexts in which science is carried out and then used; (ii) the importance of scientists' independence, transparent reasoning and use of evidence; (iii) awareness of scientists' and others' responsibilities to their communities regarding health, safety and sustainable wellbeing. This can give weighting both to understanding specific areas of science and to considering what might be done with new knowledge.

How can you enable your pupils to use schemas?

You can organise your teaching so that how schemas are used remains implicit and your pupils may not notice how their thinking is framed. As your pupils mature, they can take an explicit interest in and control how ideas are formulated. If you want your pupils to become aware of and control how they think and express themselves, schemas come to the fore.

When your pupils are at the stage of laying foundations in their practical work and understanding, you can trim and simplify. When they are ready for more, you can extend and elaborate schemas that you have in mind for them or that emerge from activities. Scope and depth can be adjusted. When your pupils are beginners in a task and when they run into difficulty, they have reasons to think about how differently they might tackle what they do. When they want to improve what they do and when they try to teach someone else, they can realise how useful it is to revise their thinking. You can help your pupils most not by asking them to treat structures as though they were rules, but by enabling them to think through what they are doing, why and how it is useful. This is how your teaching can escape mere transmission and take on a constructivist intent and influence.

Spoon-feeding your pupils with schemas as answers, making it obvious what their responses should be, does not help your pupils learn well. What your pupils think now can be a good place to start teaching ways of thinking. Assimilating and accommodating unfamiliar cognitive structures requires processing and reconstruction. For that reason, some teachers enable their pupils to display their ideas and questions at the beginning of a topic or unit and then chart what they discover – as a kind of 'learning wall' or digital file.

One strategy is to give your pupils an incomplete or jumbled picture or statement that embodies a key schema and ask them to complete or reassemble it (see Eric Lunzer's and Keith Gardner's extremely helpful *The Effective Use of Reading*, 1979, highlighting directed activities related to texts [DARTs]). These are possible exercises, all of which can be made kinaesthetic as well as visual, for example, by using cards or an interactive screen:

- cloze or gap-filling: filling in the blanks in a text or filling out the missing parts of an image;
- sequencing: putting in order sentences or images that have been mixed up;
- predicting: deciding what might come next in a series of statements or images.

Using drama as a learning medium, including physical, visual, plastic and enactive representation of thinking, offers vivid ways of experimenting with and expressing ideas. Excellent accounts of conventions such as silent tableaux, thought-tracking and hot-seating are given by Jonothan Neelands (1984) and Liz Johnson and Cecily O'Neill (1991), for example.

Here is one example. You put a question to your class. The question can be about whatever matters at that stage in the lesson: a person in history; how mountains were formed; how to work out how much fluid a cylinder holds and so on. You ask each of your pupils to stand in a line according to what they think. If they think the answer is yes, they stand at one end of a line; and if they think the answer is no, they stand at the other end. If they don't know or think it is half yes and half no, they stand in the middle, with all possible points in between. Your pupils physically show what they think by deciding where to stand. You can ask them to talk in pairs to explain their thinking and see if they change their minds. The schema embodied in the line made by your pupils represents a spectrum of views.

What can you bring into focus when you plan sequences of lessons?

The following pointers can help you plan and review your teaching. You will not want to use these all the time, but they might occasionally sharpen how you prepare sequences of lessons. The guiding force for your planning comes from your objectives, that is, your articulation of how you want your pupils to develop their thinking and what you want them to be able to do with their thinking. The clearer you can be, the better you will be able to adapt your planning in the light of their responses as lessons unfold.

Planning independent and cooperative learning with feedback

Topic/Unit title

....

Learning objectives

What do we want our pupils to think about, and what do we want them to be able to do with their thinking?

....

....

Terminology

What key words will our pupils meet and be helped to use?

....

....

Questions

What key questions will our pupils be helped to ask and answer?

....

....

Concepts

What key concepts will our pupils be helped to understand and use?

....

....

Schemas or ways of presenting ideas

What key schemas will our pupils meet and be helped to use to frame their thinking?

....

....

Strengths to build on

What capabilities and qualities do our pupils already have as a basis for this learning?

....

....

Main activities and assignments
To advance their learning, what will our pupils be doing?

....

....

Interest and relevance
How will our pupils' activities and learning connect with their interests and lives outside school?

....

....

Materials, resources, support and guidance
What will our pupils have access to? For example, technology, equipment and environments; interactions with teachers, assistants, one another and other people; sources of information; models and examples of performance to emulate and study; additional or special help.

....

....

Working with others
What activities will be cooperative, in pairs or threes, small groups and/or a large group?

....

....

Individual working
What activities will be individual, in lesson time and at home or away from school?

....

....

Feedback
What feedback will our pupils get, including for their home learning? How will they have to respond to and use their feedback?

....

....

Recording progress
How will they record what they learn and achieve?

....

....

How can you test how good your lesson planning is?

A test of your preparation and planning is to ask your pupils questions such as these:

- *How would you sum up what these lessons are about?*
- *What are these lessons meant to help you learn to do?*
- *How have you been able to build on what you already knew and skills you already had?*
- *How might what you learn in these lessons help you in life outside school?*
- *What help are you able to use in these lessons?*
- *How do you get to know how well you are doing?*
- *How do you get to improve how well you do?*
- *What have you achieved on your own, and what have you achieved working with your fellow pupils?*
- *How has your home learning helped you in these lessons?*
- *How do you record how well you do?*

How can you work on defining and refining schemas?

The clearer you and your colleagues can be about schemas that matter to your pupils' learning and how to introduce them, the better. You can help yourselves via:

- joint planning;
- peer observation;
- shared marking and moderating assessments;
- building portfolios of pupils' progress and achievement;
- in-house training and professional development.

It can be productive to share ideas in relation to questions like these:

- *When and how do we ask our pupils to show their thinking?*
- *How do our pupils get to try out new ways of thinking?*
- *What difficulties can we anticipate in developing our pupils' use of specific schemas?*
- *What signs do we look for in our pupils' developing structures for their thinking?*

Spoon-feeding may appear to be teaching, but it brings your pupils little pleasure and little genuine progression in their learning. Your pupils have to work schemas for themselves. If they do not, they may be able to repeat or reproduce something when prompted, but this is unlikely to be memorable. Your pupils' learning takes hold and can be applied when they use schemas flexibly and critically to achieve what they need or want to achieve.

See checklist C4 on pages 159–60.

Summing up

- The younger your pupils are, the more they learn through exploratory interaction with their environment. As your pupils mature, you can bring their attention to schemas by prompting them to realise what they are trying to do and how they might usefully think about it.

- School makes particular demands on your pupils' motivation, introspection and articulacy. You help them meet those demands by clarifying schemas that frame their thinking and underpin their activities. You can try to help your pupils to understand and apply the kinds of elaborate, precise schemas that are used in formal, public information.

- The learning your pupils do in relation to how they organise their thinking is likely to have greater power and be more lasting than the factual information you teach.

- The guiding force for your planning usually comes from your objectives, that is, your articulation of what you want your pupils to think about and what you want them to do with their thinking.

References

Armstrong, M. (1980) *Closely Observed Children: The Diary of a Primary Classroom*. London, UK: Writers and Readers/Chameleon.

Athey, C. (1990, 2007) *Extending Thought in Young Children: A Parent–Teacher Partnership*. London, UK: Paul Chapman Publishing.

Bartlett, F. (1932, 1997) *Remembering: A Study in Experimental and Social Psychology*. Cambridge, UK: Cambridge University Press.

Birch Farm (n.d.) 'Schemas'. www.birchfarm.co.uk/schemas.htm

Bruner, J. (1966) *Toward a Theory of Instruction*. Cambridge, MA: Harvard University Press.

Carruthers, E. and Worthington, M. (2006, 2008) *Children's Mathematics: Making Marks, Making Meaning*. London, UK: Sage Publications.

Donaldson, M. (1978) *Children's Minds*. London, UK: Fontana/Collins.

Frith, C. (2007) *Making Up the Mind: How the Brain Creates Our Mental World*. Oxford, UK: Blackwell.

Johnson, L. and O'Neill, C. (1991) *Dorothy Heathcote: Collected Writings on Education and Drama*. Evanston, IL: Northwestern University Press.

Kahneman, D. (2011) *Thinking, Fast and Slow*. London, UK: Penguin Books.

Lunzer, E. and Gardner, K. (1979) *The Effective Use of Reading*. London, UK: Heinemann Educational Books for the School Council.

McLuhan, M. (1964, 2001) *Understanding Media: The Extensions of Man*. London, UK: Routledge Classics.

Neelands, J. (1984) *Making Sense of Drama: A Guide to Classroom Practice*. London, UK: Heinemann Educational Publishers.

Piaget, J. (translated by Margaret Cook) (1952) *The Origins of Intelligence in Children*. New York: International University Press.

Ramachandran, V. (2011) *The Tell-Tale Brain: Unlocking the Mystery of Human Nature*. London, UK: Heinemann.

Rowland, S. (1984) *The Enquiring Classroom: An Introduction to Children's Learning*. London, UK: Falmer Press.

Wells, G. (1986) *The Meaning Makers: Children Learning Language and Using Language to Learn*. Portsmouth, NH: Heinemann Educational Books.

Home learning

Evidence from studies indicates that pupils can be helped to benefit from home learning and personal study as a means of developing their autonomy. In this chapter, we will look at the values of agreeing with colleagues how you will approach pupils' home learning and finding out what your pupils and their parents think about home learning. Different kinds of home-learning activities and their purposes are explored. A guide to reviewing and developing policy and practice is presented.

What counts as home learning, and what makes it an important part of your pupils' learning?

Home learning refers to things you ask your pupils to do outside lessons or activities they initiate themselves. It includes study at home, practice, projects and revision out of normal school time. For pupils who find it difficult to carry out school-related activities at home, arrangements can be made to enable them to use school facilities, such as the library or resources centre or mentored support and guidance.

Darshanand Ramdass and Barry Zimmerman (2011) reported:

> Evidence from experimental studies shows that [pupils] can be trained to develop self-regulation skills during homework activities. It is important to continue with training studies at all grade levels so that [pupils] can become aware of the relationship between homework activities and these self-regulation processes such as goals, self-efficacy, self-reflection, time management, and delay of gratification. ... Homework assignments that are adequately challenging and interesting help struggling and at-risk [pupils] develop motivation and self-regulation skills and achieve success. Teachers can help [pupils] develop

these behaviours by using homework logs. Data from the logs can help teachers show [pupils] their strengths and help them overcome their weaknesses.

(p. 195)

This would lead you to encourage your pupils to benefit from personal study as a means of pursuing their interests and aspirations through independent and collaborative enquiry and creativity.

How might you plan and use home learning?

As with many aspects of teaching, it helps if, as a team and/or as a whole school, you and your colleagues agree how you will approach independent study, practice, projects and revision. This is because pupils generally prefer to be treated fairly, and fair treatment tends to mean being treated as well as anyone who is treated well.

It also helps if, as a team and/or as a whole school, you and your colleagues regularly find out what your pupils and their parents and carers think about current practices and how they might be improved. So checking colleagues', pupils', parents' and carers' perceptions of how well school activities carried out at home contribute to your pupils' learning may prompt you to review your policy and help you develop your practice.

A log or 'planner', a kind of diary or notebook held by your pupils, enables them, their parents and carers and school personnel to exchange information, reminders, comments, and questions about requirements, activities and achievements.

It can be useful to distinguish between, on the one hand, home activities designed to reinforce and/or extend what happens in specific lessons; and, on the other hand, home activities designed to help your pupils use routines to develop their curiosity, creativity and ways of researching and revising. It is good to be clear whether any home learning activity is to:

- continue or complete work that is prompted by activities in recent lessons;
- prepare and inform activities in lessons to come;
- promote study habits and qualities that lead to success in school and beyond.

Here is an example of how a year team or subject department might explain its policy and practice. You and your colleagues can use this to review and develop what you do.

An example of a policy for home learning

1.   *We make home learning and personal study part of our planning and how we organise sequences of lessons. And we explain to our pupils why we think it is important.*

2.   *We try to make sure our pupils understand the point of every home activity or independent assignment they do.*

3.   *Usually, every week we set an activity to be done at home that should take up to about 20 minutes. This is either finishing or improving something our pupils have been doing in a lesson, or it is getting ready for an activity they are going to do in a lesson that's coming up.*

4.   *At least once a term, we ask our pupils to carry out a 'project' that runs over a few weeks. This is work they design in negotiation with us. They specify (i) What they want to achieve; (ii) What help they need; (iii) How they want their work to be responded to. Usually, they present or display these projects for peers, and sometimes other audiences, in order to learn from a range of responses and comments. We encourage them to keep this kind of work in their digital portfolios, which serve as a record of their learning and a resource for many different purposes. They have home-learning time to work on these projects.*

5.   *Usually, every week we remind our pupils that we want them to do a regular home-learning activity for about 20 minutes that involves practising and developing a routine or skill, such as reading, researching, discussing, designing, sketching, making, exercising and so on. About once a month, we spend some lesson time finding out what our pupils have been doing and suggesting ways of building on what they've been learning. This helps our pupils learn from one another as much as it helps them develop in their self-motivated and self-directed ways.*

6.   *Some of our pupils choose to do activities away from school that take longer than the estimates given above. When our pupils find home-learning activities difficult, we consult with colleagues and others about what can be done to help them. Our school runs a number of after-school clubs, for example.*

7.   *We use our school council to find out from our pupils what they think about the home learning we ask them to do and collect suggestions for ways of improving things.*

Summing up

* Your aim can be for your pupils to benefit from home learning and personal study as a way of learning how to pursue their interests and aspirations.

* Agreeing with colleagues how to approach home learning and personal study is likely to strengthen your teaching and help your pupils become effective, independent learners.

Reference

Ramdass, D. and Zimmerman, B. (2011) 'Developing self-regulation skills: The important role of homework', *Journal of Advanced Academics*, 22: 194–218.

CHAPTER 11

When to use levels or grades

Research reports that levels and grades tend to have a saccharine effect on the self-esteem of those who are usually judged to do better than their peers and to demoralise those who are judged often to do worse than their peers. It is suggested that, if you want your pupils to take notice of your marking and feedback, it is better not to give them levels or grades. When you have to make summative assessments, it is recommended that you explain which criteria and grade descriptors your pupils have satisfied and what they mean.

What does research tell us about using levels or grades in day-to-day assessments?

Levels and grades are compressed, coded versions of assessment criteria. They summarise qualities of performance and place them on a scale. They belong to summative assessments.

There has been significant research indicating that, if you want your pupils to take notice of your comments and if you want them to act on your advice, it is better not to give summative assessments. Levels and grades divert attention and energy away from learning. They can make those who come out top complacent and deflate those who fall behind.

Ruth Butler (1988) found that pupils are not helped by feedback that, in her terms, addresses pupils' egos. Seeing levels and grades diverts their motivation and depresses their achievement, even when comments are also given: 'Grades and grades plus comments had similar and generally undermining effects on both interest and performance' (p. 1). But when feedback appeals to pupils' interest in the task for its own sake, they become more engaged and do better.

That confirmed previous findings by Ruth Butler with her colleague Mordecai Nissan (1986) that pupils who feel they are doing worthwhile things and getting better at them want to do well significantly more than pupils whose main concern is wanting to have badges of approval:

> *Intrinsic motivation ... depends on the dynamic interaction between the stimulus and the individual, i.e., on the degree to which a task continues to be perceived as challenging and as providing satisfying increments in one's knowledge about one's competence.*

(p. 210)

This is in keeping with research carried out over several decades by Carol Dweck and her colleagues. Claudia Mueller and Dweck (1998) asked 128 10- and 11-year-old children to solve a series of mathematical problems. The first exercises were simple and, on completing these, each child was given one sentence of praise. Some were praised for their intellect (*You did really well, you're so clever*), and others for their hard work (*You did really well, you must have tried really hard*). Then the children were given more challenging problems. What happened was dramatic. The pupils who had been praised for their effort were more willing to try new approaches. They were more resilient and tended to say that the failures they had were because they had not tried hard enough. The pupils who had been praised for their cleverness worried more about failure, tended to choose tasks that did not stretch them, rarely took risks and gave up sooner when the problems got harder. When the pupils were asked to write to children in another school about what they had experienced, some of the ones who had been praised for being clever lied about their scores, saying they had done better than they had.

The challenge for you as a teacher is to promote and model intrinsic rather than extrinsic motivation and satisfaction. To achieve this, you and your colleagues have to work on enabling your pupils to internalise the purposes and audiences for their work and to subordinate their interest in levels and grades to their wanting to achieve standards they set themselves and recognise as valid.

It can be a problem that you are required, or feel obliged, to keep your pupils and other people regularly informed about grades. When you want or have to make assessments summative, explain what the marks and codes mean in words your pupils can understand. When you want your pupils to use assessments to help them learn and achieve standards they strive for, avoid levels and grades.

Summing up

- If you want your pupils to take notice of your marking and feedback, it is better not to give them levels or grades.

- When you give summative assessments using scores, levels or grades, explain to your pupils which criteria and grade descriptors they have satisfied, and what they can do to make further progress.

References

Butler, R. (1988) 'Enhancing and undermining intrinsic motivation', *British Journal of Educational Psychology*, 58: 1–14.

Butler, R. and Nissan, M. (1986) 'Effects of no feedback, task-related commands, and grades on intrinsic motivation and performance', *Journal of Educational Psychology*, 78: 210–216.

Mueller, C. and Dweck, C. (1998) 'Praise for intelligence can undermine children's motivation and performance', *Journal of Personality and Social Psychology*, 75, 1: 33–52.

CHAPTER 12

Developing effective feedback for your pupils

In this chapter, different kinds of feedback and feedforward are analysed and illustrated. A grid is given which you can use to explore who gives feedback, what targets and criteria are used, and what happens next. A similar grid is provided to help you review how effectively your pupils use their feedback. Differences between formative and summative assessments are examined according to their agents, purposes, criteria and outcomes. Different kinds of targets and criteria are explained. A draft policy for written feedback is presented for you to critique and adapt.

What is feedback, and how can it help your pupils?

Feedback consists of responses to and evaluations of pupils' efforts: informal impressions as well as formal assessments. Ideally, feedback informs and motivates. Pupils can give themselves feedback; they can give one another feedback; you and your assistants can give your pupils feedback; and so too can other people who become audiences for or users of your pupils' work. Feedback can help you and your pupils make decisions about what to do next. It can help you and your pupils talk about what you need to do to encourage, guide and support their learning.

Before feedback, there can be feedforward. Feedforward gives pupils information about what they are going to do. When their activity is underway, the feedforward they remember reminds them of what they are trying to do. As well as being told about upcoming activities, pupils can create their own feedforward, envisaging for themselves and with others what they are going to do and how they will set about it. This is akin to sports people's visualising their performance.

Feedback tells pupils about how well they are doing in relation to what they are trying to do. It is all the richer if it builds on good feedforward. It helps pupils answer questions that promote learning, such as, *What am I getting better at? What can I work on now?* The closer their feedback and feedforward to their activity, the likelier it is to benefit their learning. The younger your pupils are and the fewer they are in number, the more their feedback and feedforward can be part of talking about ongoing activities.

Research (e.g. John Hattie and Helen Timperley, 2007) has shown that the quality of your pupils' feedback might determine their success more than any other single facet of teaching. This is a litmus test: do assessments lead to decisions and actions that help your pupils learn? Formative assessments are designed to help them during activities; summative assessments report judgements that are usually made at a remove from the event.

Feedback helps your pupils reflect on and improve their performance, when it:

- refers to the purpose of activity;
- is given and received during the activity or as close to it as possible;
- uses language your pupils can understand;
- enables your pupils to build on what they do well;
- is clear enough to be responded to;
- is not allowed to be part of a dull routine but is expressed with genuine interest and consequence;
- informs dialogue between your pupils and with you and those who are there to help;
- is varied, sometimes low key, sometimes intensive, often spoken, sometimes written;
- assists self- and peer assessment;
- picks out what the learner has done well and is learning to do better;
- may refer to a small number of essential criteria or targets.

The best kinds of feedback shift your pupils' attention away from thinking about their abilities as though they were innate and unchanging and towards thinking about what they are aiming to achieve and how their present effort compares with previous ones. This can happen naturally as part of spontaneous and voluntary activity and learning. As part of the taught curriculum, though, it is for you to make opportunities for feedback and feedforward to inform what your pupils do, promoting intrinsic enjoyment and interest in learning.

There is valuable research (e.g. by Carol Dweck, 2000) suggesting that extrinsic motivations and rewards undermine confidence, autonomy and participation. Your pupils learn more and better, and so feel better about themselves and their learning, when they see that success comes from effort and resourcefulness, which they can control, rather than from innate ability or reliance on others, which they cannot control.

These are the kinds of things your pupils might say and how you and teaching assistants might respond.

Dialogue promoting constructive attitudes and actions

Your pupils say:	You say:
I can't do it.	Can you try it a different way? Or Perhaps try one more time, and then we can talk some more.
What do I have to do?	Let me see what you have done so far. Or What's your plan?
Can you do this for me?	Remind me what the next thing to do is. Or May I try to help you?
I'm no good at this.	But you're good at … . Let's see if we can build on that. Or, It may be hard now, but you will improve if you keep trying to ….
I don't like this. It's boring.	Remind me what the point of this is. Or, What it leads to gets more interesting – trust me.
I can't do this. I give up.	Do you want to look at how other people tackle this? Or, This is a new challenge for all of us, so don't expect it to be easy.
I'll never be any good.	I don't agree. You can try to be the best you can be at this. Or, What help do you need? Remember how hard you tried on … .
I've done this before.	What did you do well last time? It's good to try improving on past performances, isn't it? Or Can you see ways of developing this further?
This is too easy for me.	I can make it more challenging. Are you up for this? Or Could you help ____ who isn't finding it so easy?

What kinds of feedback can you arrange for your pupils to use?

Feedback can be *shown* as a 'recipe' or diagram or demonstration or model to follow. Feedback can be *spoken*. If it is appropriate for your pupils' stage of development, feedback can be *written*.

The better your pupils come to understand what they can aim for and different ways of going about it, the better they learn. Examples of pupils' work, in progress or as a final performance, are a good way of showing *This is how someone else tackled what you are trying to do.* Body language and gestures also communicate responses to and guidance about what your pupils do. Ways of giving spoken or written feedback include praising, asking questions and giving constructive critiques and advice. You can use the grid below to analyse feedback.

Analysing examples of your pupils' feedback

Kind of feedback	By whom? When?	Using whose targets or criteria?	Looking forward and/or back?	What happens next?
Shown:				
Spoken:				
Written:				

These are some of the possibilities.

By whom? For example:

- one or more peers;
- you and/or your assistants;
- another audience, a participant, professional, expert or coach.

When? For example:

- before the activity: to prepare and set up activity in a lesson or unit (*What do I know? What do I want to know? What can I already do? What shall I learn to do?*);
- during the activity: briefly taking stock of progress and looking for improvement (*What is going well? What am I getting better at? What can I improve?*);
- after the activity: reviewing how well things were done (*How good was that? What standard have I reached?*).

Using whose targets or criteria? For example:

- a pupil's own;
- peers';
- yours and/or assistants';

- an audience's, participant's, professional's, expert's or coach's;
- borrowed from, or simulating, a real-life or hypothetical context (e.g. *To improve the layout of our car-park ...*; *We'll work as if in a television studio/ chemical laboratory/...*);
- the national curriculum's, an examination board's or a commercial scheme's.

Looking forward and/or back? For example, looking back at:

- what she or he is doing better than before;
- what she or he has done that is right or matches a criterion or meets a standard.

For example, looking forward to:

- how to get better at what she or he is doing;
- how to learn better.

What happens next? For example, the pupil:

- carries on with or changes what she or he is doing;
- gives a response in dialogue;
- feels encouraged and fulfilled, or begins to rethink her or his approach, and perhaps starts something new;
- makes a record of progress;
- has an award or celebration.

For example, you:

- stick with or change what you planned;
- make a mental note to find out more;
- feel pleased or encouraged or begin to rethink your approach;
- realise what additional teaching, or what adjustment to teaching, might be needed;
- make a record of progress;
- decide an award or celebration is called for.

What you want to look for is variety and fitness for purpose. You can use the following grid to review how effective various kinds and instances of feedback have been.

Evaluating your pupils' feedback and planning for even better

Name of pupil or teaching group: ....   *Date of review: ....*

Kind of feedback	What has worked well, and how do we know?	What has been less effective, and what can we do about it?
Shown:		
....		
....		
....		
Spoken:		
....		
....		
....		
Written:		
....		
....		
....		

You want to build on your pupils' perceptions and help them benefit from their assessments. You can say, for example: *In this next activity you're going to decide what counts as good work. You and a partner are going to assess yourselves, using targets or criteria I give you as well as ones you decide on. Afterwards you're going to say what difference, if any, it made to how much you enjoyed and how well you did the activity. We're going to use this experience to make sure you get the kind of feedback that helps you learn and do well.* And, of course, you should keep your promise and help your pupils periodically to review how useful their feedback is.

How do summative and formative assessments differ? How can targets and criteria be used to guide and support your pupils' learning?

The feedback a pupil gets can help her or him answer the summative question *How well have I done?* With that information, your pupils may move on to the next task or stage of their learning, repeat the assessment, leave the course they are on, leave the institution they are in or leave education altogether.

The feedback a pupil gets can help her or him answer the formative question *How well am I doing?* Having received that information, your pupils are better placed to continue learning and develop further.

Summative and formative assessments differ in respect of purpose, outcome, who does the evaluating and the choice of targets or criteria.

Differences between summative and formative assessments

	Purposes and outcomes	Assessors	Criteria
Summative assessments	inform reports of capability and qualifications	are publicly authorised examiners	are relatively stable; express or are derived from public standards
Formative assessments	as far as possible lead to more and better learning	are pupils, teachers and anyone who comments on pupils' work	are variable and dynamic; are likely to be task and context specific and can include any that pupils and teachers think could promote learning

An obstacle to your pupils' turning feedforward and feedback into improved performance is that, if you judge them or they judge themselves by decontextualised, fragmented criteria, they are diverted from grasping the totality of high-quality work. Would-be universal criteria do not help your pupils to tailor their ideas about what might be 'right' or 'good' to the tasks and problems they face. They can be lulled into feeling they have only to do what they have been told to do, and then they feel clueless when they have to adapt to particular circumstances and think for themselves.

Targets and criteria come to life when your pupils use them to work out and plan what to do. Using formative targets and criteria helps them learn to:

- diagnose strengths and weaknesses in their own and others' performance;
- decide what teaching and support they would like to help them;
- devise targets and criteria for their activities.

You can control how you assess your pupils' learning in lessons.

Formative assessment's role is to inform and enhance pupils' learning. It can address the quality of teaching, resources and the learning environment. It can refer to the pupils' attitudes, motivations and readiness to tackle tasks. It does not have to wait till the end of a course, nor does it need to be carried out under controlled conditions. It does not have to involve writing, nor be sent away to be marked with a delay of many weeks before results are known. It does not have to be recorded or monitored. It can be quality assured in the same way that teaching and learning can be.

There is extensive research evidence that attending to formative processes significantly enhances success in summative assessments (see Black and Wiliam, 1998; and Black *et al.*, 2003). But there is no necessity for formative processes to detract from the achievement of competitive standards through summative assessments. It tends rather to be the case that preoccupation with summative evaluation weakens formative feedback and can be counter-productive even in its own terms.

What does a useful policy for pupils' written feedback look like?

It is common for conscientious teachers to feel guilty about the marking they do. You can easily feel you should do more, but you cannot sustain working a 60-hour-plus week. You need to take care to lead a healthy, balanced life. Unfortunately, it can happen that some teachers ramp up the pressure by boasting about or exaggerating how much they do, how late they stay at school, as though there were a competition to be the hardest working. What matters more than the hours you spend marking or the length of comments you write is that your pupils make practical use of your feedback and are encouraged by the example you set through your marking to engage with what they do and try to do their best.

If your pupils are able to learn through your writing to them, you might like to consider the following approach. Originally developed in the 1990s during a residential training conference, its purpose was to resolve long-running differences of opinion amongst members of staff at Saint Osmund's Middle School, Dorchester, Dorset, the United Kingdom (UK), about how best to mark their pupils' work. The senior leadership team wanted staff members collectively to argue through their contrasting approaches. They succeeded by inviting everyone in their teaching teams to improve a draft policy statement and having each team in turn present its conclusions, build on one another's ideas and finally come to a consensus. Since then, a good number of schools have used it as a basis for clarifying their principles and practices. What would you omit? What would you amend? What would you add?

Example of a policy for pupils' written feedback

- *Written feedback, like spoken feedback, focuses as often as possible on what our pupils are doing better, and on what they can do next to develop further.*
- *Our pupils know the purpose of their activities and look for feedback on that.*
- *When we mark their work, they know when they can expect it to be returned and the kinds of things they will have to do as follow-up.*
- *Our pupils also assess their own and one another's work.*
- *Comments are linked to what our pupils are trying to do, to lesson objectives, to individual pupils' targets and to public assessment criteria, especially when preparing for formal tests or qualifications.*

- *Comments are personalised, for example, addressing the individual or group members by name; are positive in overall tone; focus on progress; and constructively indicate next steps.*
- *We sometimes correct single errors, but we routinely look for opportunities to teach patterns, key skills and schematic thinking.*
- *Our pupils understand the meaning and purpose of symbols, codes, scores, levels or grades, when these are used.*
- *More often than not, our pupils have time, and help if they need it, to do something with the marking they receive. They follow up their feedback: for example, by finishing off, making corrections, looking at someone else's work, producing an improved version, practising certain skills, developing the work in certain directions and so on.*
- *Our pupils use special notebooks or pages in their exercise books to collect word families or concepts, information webs, algorithms, reminders, revision notes and so on.*
- *Correction or proofreading looks like this:*

✓ in the margin	means, *That's right* or *interesting* or *to the point.*
→ in the margin	means, *Look along this line to find something to put right.*
— (underlining of pupil's work)	means, *This needs improving.*
Words in the margin	mean, *I have put something right for you to learn from.*
Comments at the end	lead our pupils to take action by way of follow-up, always with the purpose of developing their learning.

See checklist C6 on page 160.

Summing up

- Assessments that are part of your teaching lead to decisions and actions which encourage, guide and support your pupils' learning.
- Your pupils learn more and better when they see that success depends on effort and resourcefulness, which they can control, rather than on innate ability or what other people tell them, which they cannot control.
- Your pupils learn and do well when they have time, and help if they need it, to do something with the feedback they get.

References

Black, P., Harrison, C., Lee, C., Marshall, B. and Wiliam, D. (2003) *Assessment for Learning: Putting It into Practice.* Buckingham, UK: Open University Press.

Black, P. and Wiliam, D. (1998) 'Assessment and classroom learning', *Assessment In Education*, 5, 1: 7–74.

Dweck, C. S. (2000) *Self-Theories: Their Role in Motivation, Personality, and Development.* Philadelphia, PA: Psychology Press.

Hattie, J. and Timperley, H. (2007), 'The power of feedback', *Review of Educational Research*, 77, 1: 81–112. http://education.qld.gov.au/staff/development/performance/resources/readings/power-feedback.pdf.

CHAPTER 13

Charting your pupils' progress and showing their achievements

In this chapter, we will explore the role and value of your pupils' collecting examples of their work. These can serve to illustrate their progress and help them and you survey, summarise and report their achievements.

What traces of their activities can your pupils collect?

You can teach in such a way that your pupils keep examples of what they do, including commentaries and reflections. Seeing where they have come from can help them think about where they would like to take their activities and learning. Though it may be practical in some cases for you to store their work, it is most helpful if you signal that their collected and sampled work belongs to them. You can help them appreciate that your having access to their folders and books informs how you teach them.

Your pupils can collect prototypes, drafts, experiments, trials and products arising from their activities:

- notes, sketches, rehearsals and so on for work in progress;
- assignments, performances, investigations, solutions, presentations, publications, artefacts, projects, reports and so on, which they present as completed work;

and comments on their work:

- their self-assessments and reflections;
- other people's responses, for example, those of peers, real audiences and visitors;
- your feedback and dialogue with them.

Comments on your pupils' work can identify:

- areas of learning in which they have made notable progress;
- notable achievements in personal terms and attainments in academic terms.

How does keeping track of your pupils' achievements help them and you?

Over time, your pupils can select and annotate examples of their work as a record of their experiences and achievements. Keeping digital, paper-based and physical testimony to their efforts assists ongoing learning and occasions when reports and decisions about next steps in education are wanted.

When summaries need to be made, you and your pupils can survey their collected work and comments and make sense of their achievements for any interested party. When it is feasible and ethical for pupils to have a voice in formal reporting, they can contribute and be joint or autobiographical authors. Some schools begin this process as soon as possible, enabling pupils to show their work to their parents when they come into school to find out about what their children have been doing.

Keeping track of their work can feed into your:

- ongoing dialogue between you and your pupils, as well as with parents and others;
- deciding how to carry on developing their knowledge, skill and understanding;
- judgements about what assessment criteria have been met, what targets have been hit and what standards have been met;
- report writing;
- meetings with parents and carers;
- case conferences;
- annual reviews and transition meetings;
- testimonials and references.

(See leading researcher–writers on the assessment and recording of pupils' achievements, e.g. Wynne Harlen *et al.*,1992.)

Summing up

- Your teaching can enable your pupils to trace their activities and learning by keeping examples of their work, including comments and reflections.
- You and your pupils can view the collected material when, jointly or separately, you want or need to give accounts of achievements and make decisions about progress, prospects and plans.

Reference

Harlen, W., Gipps, C., Broadfoot, P. and Nuttall, D. (1992) 'Assessment and the improvement of education', *The Curriculum Journal*, 3, 2: 215–230.

Moderating assessments

Effective moderation meetings enable you and your colleagues to:

- check your pupils have valid opportunities to show their capabilities;
- seek consensus about what your pupils have to do to match given criteria and achieve prescribed standards;
- standardise your assessments;
- help your pupils improve their chances of success;
- develop portfolios representing a range of pupils' achievements.

This entails examining your prejudices, assumptions, values and insights by comparing one another's perceptions of strengths and weaknesses in pupils' work. This chapter offers you a protocol for moderation meetings, along with recommendations about keeping portfolios of pupils' assessed work.

What does moderating assessments mean?

Moderating assessments is what markers and examiners do to standardise national test results and qualifications. You and your colleagues can similarly meet to discuss images, models, writing and so on that your pupils have produced. When there are no visible or tangible outcomes from their activities, you can listen to one another's accounts of what pupils said, gestured, signed and did, and you might view photos or film clips. You are in a position to know more about your pupils and their activities than distant assessors do, but when deciding what levels or grades to award them, you work within a framework of public standards.

As you try to verify that you are applying criteria fairly and accurately, differences in colleagues' assumptions and attitudes inevitably come to the surface. Meetings are an opportunity to explore those. In the public arena, the chief examiner has ultimately to determine standards, whereas your team can be free to seek consensus. More than that, the process permits you to share your teaching methods, experiences and knowledge.

Moderation meetings can be designed to enable you and your colleagues to:

- check that your pupils have proper opportunities to show what they know, understand and can do in relation to prescribed criteria and requirements for qualifications;
- reassure yourselves that your summative judgement making avoids personal bias and is consistent;
- clear up confusions and misconceptions about curriculum and assessment requirements, and come to as much of a consensus as you can about what criteria mean and what counts as having achieved standards;
- see what your pupils need to do to improve their chances of success;
- collect examples of your pupils' activities and the standards they achieve for you, your pupils and others to refer to.

If you have no immediate colleagues in your school with whom you can compare assessments, you might find opportunities to meet teachers from other schools or in a subject association to see how close your perspectives and perceptions are to theirs. In a secondary school, you might show colleagues who teach subjects other than yours what you do and find out about what they do in relation to standardising assessments. You might sometimes join their meetings and show them how you have assessed work that might relate to their subjects.

How can developing portfolios of your pupils' activities help you improve the validity and usefulness of your assessments?

Paul Black *et al.* (2010) suggested that you can strengthen the validity of your assessments by:

- carrying out conscientious in-house moderation exercises;
- discussing with your colleagues what you want your pupils to aim for;
- building and sharing portfolios of pupils' activities to illustrate criteria and standards.

They concluded that 'the development of a portfolio approach [is] effective in giving teachers scope to reconstruct their practices, whilst the scrutiny required by a discipline of moderation provide[s] a structure in which professional development in summative assessment [can] be achieved through collegial interaction'

(p. 227). They recommended that portfolios contain evidence of many different kinds, taken from activities in all sorts of circumstances, shapes and media, 'in order to enhance validity, and to generate a more critical approach towards the use of tests'. They suggested that 'conventional tests, whether generated internally or from external sources, might well form a component of such portfolios'. They reported that portfolios 'could be exchanged and discussed both between teachers in the same school, and … between schools' (p. 215).

The essential components of such portfolios are that, in your year or subject team or department, you:

- decide what counts as valid and reliable assessment, over time using as many different kinds of work produced by pupils in as many different contexts as is feasible and consistent with your curriculum planning;
- devise and follow rigorous, transparent procedures for moderating sample portfolios in your school and, if possible, across schools;
- use portfolios as a way of sharing information about your pupils' achievements with the pupils themselves, their parents, governors and others.

Moderation meetings are a process, and portfolios are a product. Over time, moderation meetings should benefit your pupils' ongoing learning while securing accurate judgements about what they achieve when those are called for. Portfolios embody your team's efforts to do justice to your pupils' capabilities and be publicly accountable for your work.

A possible policy statement and guide to practice for keeping examples of their assessed work

What our pupils achieve is illustrated in portfolios of their work which:

- *Draw on our pupils' own personal work-files to represent their capabilities as fairly and diversely as possible*
- *Show our pupils, their parents, governors and other interested parties the kinds of activities our pupils engage in and the standards they achieve*
- *Enable us to discuss teaching, learning and assessment within our teams, with our colleagues on cross-curricular projects, with trainee teachers, colleagues from local schools and other interested parties*
- *Show visiting authorities, including inspectors, how rigorously we use assessment criteria and verify standards*

How can you and your colleagues manage your moderation meetings?

Having a moderation meeting each term is a good way of introducing yourselves to one another, of welcoming new colleagues and of refreshing everyone's subject knowledge and teaching capabilities. If the team you work in has not had a moderation meeting for over a year, you probably need to have one. There is no substitute for looking together at what your pupils achieve.

It is helpful if at least one colleague circulates in advance, or brings to the meeting, copies of pupils' work and relevant assessment criteria. Everyone has to work together, comparing one another's perceptions of strengths and weaknesses in your pupils' work. This allows each of you to uncover something of your prejudices, assumptions, values, insights and interpretations.

Until you have established effective routines, it could be useful for someone other than the colleague presenting pupils' work to lead your meeting. This is a facilitative rather than a directive role, with a focus on building colleagues' confidence in their combined ability to arrive at fair, justifiable assessments.

Here is an example of a protocol for moderation meetings, based on practice developed by Daphne Wright and colleagues at Portsdown Primary School in Portsmouth, the United Kingdom (UK). It is worth noting that at the time I visited them, these colleagues had developed their shared assessment practices so well that they were barely conscious of having a protocol. This shows how it is possible to be implicitly skilled and only to need explicit processes for new colleagues or when changed circumstances require it.

An example of a protocol for moderating assessments of pupils' activities

Part 1

- *As a group, we agree what assessment criteria we will use and which of us will present pupils' activities for discussion.*
- *The presenting teacher describes or shows examples of pupils' activities, indicating the background, strengths and weaknesses.*
- *The rest of the group asks the presenting teacher about her or his thinking, for the time being leaving aside the question of what level or grade the examples might represent.*

Part 2

- *As a group, we thank the presenting teacher, who sits back while the rest of us discuss the examples and ways of judging them.*
- *We use what we know about the context for the activities, similar pupils' progress, official standards and formal criteria to discuss the examples' merits and weaknesses without assigning levels or grades.*
- *Then, as a whole group, we come to a consensus or majority view about what levels or grades we propose.*

Part 3

- *As a whole group, we explore next steps in learning for the pupil/s we have discussed and implications for our teaching.*
- *We decide whether to include any of the examples with levels or grades in a portfolio of assessed work.*
- *We summarise what we have learned and what implications there might be for our teaching and our pupils' learning.*

You want to become conscious of factors that affect judgement making. This translates into specific ways of speaking and listening. You can think about how best to help one another answer questions like these:

Questions to ask as part of your moderation exercises

Can we make a list of the strengths we see in these examples?
Can we match these examples to specific assessment criteria?
Can we say what these examples' salient features are? How can we justify our judgements?
Can we see where a pupil falls short of what is required for a specific award?
Can we take account of how the context and conditions might have affected what the pupil/s did without jeopardising the validity and reliability of our assessments?
Can we explain what each pupil would have to do to qualify for the next level or grade up the scale?
Can we outline the teaching that could help our pupils make progress?

How can you try to make sure your moderation meetings benefit your team, hence your pupils?

You can review how successful your moderation processes are when you and your colleagues:

- find out from your pupils how well prepared they feel they are for their formal assessments;
- find out how well you and your colleagues can point to evidence of your pupils' satisfying specific assessment criteria;
- share ways of helping your pupils use their feedback and assessments;
- check that your moderation practices are as good as those of other teams in your school and elsewhere;
- check what you are learning individually and as a team about your teaching and your pupils' learning.

See checklist C7 on pages 160–1.

Summing up

- In a moderation exercise, you and your colleagues analyse examples of pupils' activities and try to agree what standards they represent.
- The process of moderation enables you and your colleagues to develop how you approach your teaching and your pupils' learning by exploring your understanding of assessment criteria and performance standards.
- You and your colleagues can use portfolios of pupils' work to do justice to your pupils' capabilities and take some public accountability for their results.

Reference

Black, P., Harrison, C., Hodgen, J., Marshall, B. and Serret, N. (2010) 'Validity in teachers' summative assessments', *Assessment in Education: Principles, Policy & Practice*, 17: 215–232.

Job satisfaction and continuing to learn about teaching

Making meetings useful

Meetings in school matter because they affect how you and your colleagues feel about your work and how well you provide for your pupils. In this chapter, there are recommendations about how meetings can be chaired effectively. It is suggested that each agenda item's specific purpose be made clear. Guidance will be given about what to avoid and what to focus on.

Why are meetings important?

Successful teaching and learning rely on your looking inward and outward in critically constructive ways. Morale and energy depend on relationships, and relationships are developed or thwarted in meetings. In their excellent opinion piece 'Managing to lead?' Alma Harris and Michelle Jones (2012) wrote that: 'Essentially, management is about maintenance – keeping things running efficiently, effectively and well', and meetings are a principal means of maintaining morale, direction and focus, but only if everyone present communicates openly.

Well-run meetings and good routines facilitate constructive relationships and open communication, both of which are vital to high-quality performance and job satisfaction. In their research into attitudes to error, stress and teamwork, J. Bryan Sexton *et al.* (2000) reported that: 'Highly effective cockpit crews use one third of their communications to discuss threats and errors in their environment, regardless of their workload, whereas poor performing teams spend about 5% of their time doing the same.' A key benefit of efficient communication is that colleagues deal with envisaged and actual:

- barriers to their effective working;
- shortcomings and mistakes;
- risks and threats.

Your meetings can be designed to enable your team to do your best for your pupils. The better your meetings do that, the more likely you are to enjoy your work and continue to learn about it. Managers and leaders have a key role in establishing a beneficial ethos and effective routines, but you cannot rely on them to run all of your meetings. Those who attend can govern how meetings are run. What you discuss often reflects authorities and interests beyond the group, but how you balance your agendas with theirs is for you to decide. The better you communicate with your leaders and managers, the more effective your team and your organisation will be.

It is valuable to open your meetings to people who are touched by matters dealt with there. Everyone's sense of shared interest is enhanced through attendance or systems of representation. For example, what might governors or other partners gain from and/or contribute to your meetings? How might you ask researchers, consultants or inspectors to engage with your information sharing, discussions and decision-making? How might members of the school council or other pupils usefully contribute?

How can meetings be made meaningful?

It can happen that people come with matters at the front of their minds that could be an obstacle to everyone's getting what they should from their meeting. So it can be a useful strategy for the person convening or chairing to give some space, before the meeting proper starts, for relatively informal talk. Without taking too much time from the meeting itself, and if this has a prospect of being beneficial, questions or issues arising from initial, informal talk can be summarised, noted and, if appropriate, forwarded to those who might help clarify or give a response. Then everyone can get down to business.

An agenda needs to be available to everyone, making clear what items are to be addressed. It helps for everyone to be clear about what a meeting, or any part of a meeting, is intended to achieve. For example, is it for everyone present to:

- be informed about something?
- discuss something?
- decide something?

Clarifying this can transform the quality of meetings.

As you address any item, everyone should know:

- *Are we going to talk about this?*
- *If yes, for how long?*
- *Are there practical consequences to this? If, yes, what do we want them to be?*

To help take stock of your meetings, you and your colleagues can share perceptions, asking, for example,

Do our meetings:

- *have a clear purpose?*
- *achieve what they're meant to achieve?*
- *finish on time?*

Factors contributing to successful meetings include making sure:

- as many people as possible or representatives have a voice in deciding the agenda;
- anyone who has a particular role to play understands what their contribution will be;
- everyone knows what they need to bring with them, or has received documentation beforehand, or has sight of it during the meeting;
- the meeting is scheduled for a suitable place with feasible start and finish times, and the meeting place is comfortable, equipped, arranged so that people can see one another and provided with water and refreshments;
- the meeting place is left fit and ready for whoever will use it next.

These are some things to avoid and some things to test and see if they make a difference:

To avoid ...	Whenever possible ...
Automatically having the most senior or powerful person chair the meeting	Enable different people to act as chair, whose job is to: – achieve what the meeting is meant to achieve – make sure everyone keeps to the point – give everyone who wants to speak the chance to do so – keep to time
Ignoring the context of your meeting and its relevance to events	Make connections between this meeting and other activities and processes in your school
having the same format for all your meetings	Vary the kinds of activity, for example, change seating to suit the meeting's or item's purpose and enable different people to be the focus of attention; when it is useful, ask people to read an important text, to talk in twos or threes, and pool ideas as a whole group; and so on
Assuming everyone knows what the meeting or agenda item is for	Thank people for coming and briefly state what you aim to achieve; and make clear whether each item is intended to give information, invite discussion, or lead to a decision

Continued

expecting that giving information leads to its being understood and acted on	enable whoever will be responsible for subsequent action to voice their understanding of what is stated, discussed or decided
letting distractions divert the meeting from its purpose	arrange for issues that arise, but which are not part of the agenda, to be addressed elsewhere
delegating tasks to people who are not present or who have not been involved	make sure the people who are responsible for the matter being addressed are at the meeting and committed to what is stated, discussed or decided
overrunning	keep to time
leaving the meeting without record or consequence	record key points, conclusions and recommendations, for example, using an interactive whiteboard or flipchart; and agree what should happen next
taking colleagues' time and efforts for granted	make sure individuals or teams are thanked for specific contributions and everyone is thanked for taking part

See checklist C2 on pages 158–9.

Summing up

- Morale, commitment and energy depend on relationships, and relationships are developed in meetings.

- What you discuss in meetings often reflects authorities and interests beyond the group, but how you balance your agendas with theirs is for you to decide.

- The effectiveness of meetings is transformed by everyone's being clear about what a meeting, or any part of a meeting, is intended to achieve, whether it be to give information, to discuss something or to decide something.

References

Harris, A. and Jones, M. (2012) 'Managing to lead?' Nottingham, UK: National College for School Leadership. www.nationalcollege.org.uk/cm-mc-let-op-harrisjones.pdf.

Sexton, J. B., Thomas, E. J. and Helmreich, R. L. (2000) 'Error, stress, and teamwork in medicine and aviation: Cross sectional surveys', *The British Medical Journal*, 320, 7237: 745–749.

Job enrichment

Job satisfaction is how you feel about your experience. It is seen to depend on having well-defined roles and responsibilities; on having forums and channels of communication which provide encouragement, guidance and support; and on having achievements acknowledged and communicated. Job enrichment is an enhancement of your experience and is seen to depend on having scope for personal achievement and its recognition, increasingly challenging and responsible work and opportunities for individual growth and advancement. It might be said that job satisfaction is your responsibility and that job enrichment is your management's and leadership's responsibility, though the two are intertwined. A checklist is given to help you reflect on your experience. Conditions for a school's effectiveness as an organisation and for individuals' and teams' autonomous and cooperative development are explained.

How can you and your colleagues benefit by being challenged to take increasing responsibility in your work?

Psychologists and consultants Frederick Herzberg, Bill Paul and Keith Robertson (1968) have much to offer. Their key concepts are:

- performance: how well you do your job;
- motivation: whatever spurs you toward doing well enough to feel satisfaction and gain recognition;
- satisfaction: the sense you have of doing your job well;
- recognition: being appreciated for what you do;
- enrichment: experiencing changes in your working environment that help you feel motivated and gain recognition for your efforts.

The American Herzberg and his British-based colleagues Paul and Robertson (1968) wrote that 'job enrichment improves both task efficiency and human satisfaction by means of building into people's jobs, quite specifically, greater scope for personal achievement and its recognition, more challenging and responsible work, and more opportunities for individual advancement and growth' (p. 73).

These are three foundation stones for job satisfaction and job enrichment:

- defining roles and tasks;
- maintaining forums and channels of communication which provide guidance and support;
- acknowledging and communicating achievements.

Defining roles and tasks

Having a clear job description and keeping it up to date are essential to your enjoying your work and doing your job well. If there are ambiguities or uncertainties, those concerned have to work together to clarify whose job is what. This may seem obvious, but it is troubling how often people do not know what is expected of them and what they are aiming to achieve.

Maintaining forums and channels of communication

Having ways of sharing information, experiences and ideas is essential to your being able to teach well and develop through your work. Typical contexts are:

- regular team meetings where successes, problems and solutions are discussed;
- supervision, mentoring, coaching, training and action research;
- information about what colleagues in your school and beyond achieve and are developing.

These provide you with essential guidance, support and feedback.

Acknowledging and communicating achievements

Your sustained performance and growth depend on how your pupils' achievements, and your part in them, are acknowledged and communicated. Typical ways of doing this are:

- records of your professional development and its impact, which inform annual reviews and references to support internal promotion or external applications;
- intranet and/or internet sites and/or other means of disseminating activities, including your school's self-evaluations, reports to governors and publications.

Your job satisfaction depends on having opportunities to grow as a person and to further your career. You can agree with colleagues, managers and leaders how you will develop, for example via:

- work-shadowing;
- specialising in teaching certain groups of pupils and areas of learning;
- extending the range of pupils and areas of learning you teach;
- contributing to and/or leading developmental projects, for example, in developing uses of new teaching methods, technologies and resources;
- working with colleagues in your school and elsewhere, for example, engaging in peer observations, team teaching and developing cross-curricular cooperation;
- guiding and supporting colleagues;
- collecting, interpreting and using pupils' perceptions of lessons and school life;
- liaising with organisations beyond your school, such as professional networks, associations and examination boards;
- communicating with partners in the community and professional and research organisations.

Highlighted by Herzberg and his colleagues, 'The message of both theory and practice is that people respond cautiously to new responsibility; they feel their way and seek advice' (1968, p. 74). When people are given the chance to achieve more, they might not take the chance, but there is no reason for them to achieve less. Managers lose nothing, and have everything to gain, by trying to enable colleagues' motivation and satisfaction to grow. Wise and skilled leadership is called for. If the necessary intelligence and commitment to devolve responsibilities are lacking, it can easily happen that your professional relationships and effectiveness fall prey to overbearing government legislation, interfering micro-management, ill-constructed target-setting, punitive inspection regimes and unproductive changes to schools' foundations and governance.

How might your school enhance job enrichment?

Surveying job enrichment

How well do you and your colleagues:	Where is this evident?	Why might this be something to work on?	What can be done to enrich this?
• Understand what your roles and main tasks are?			
• Get guidance, support and feedback?			
• Have your work appreciated and recognised?			
• Have opportunities to do more responsible and challenging work?			
• Have opportunities to develop personally and progress in your career?			

There is consistent evidence that job enrichment brings gains in satisfaction and performance when 'management becomes a service, its purpose to enable, encourage, assist, and reinforce achievement by employees' (Herzberg *et al.*, 1968, p. 77). When responsibility is put squarely with the people doing the job, they need and want feedback. A school's health and effectiveness as an organisation depend less on there being communication 'downward' from managers to staff members and far more on consultation 'upward'. Under these conditions, managers and leaders get accurate feedback on individuals' strengths and weaknesses, capabilities, interests and potentials. This inspires and informs the development of a thriving organisation that depends on everyone's having authentic, motivating work and on everyone's being well managed and led: 'When these conditions are met, the job itself becomes a true learning situation, its ingredients the motivators' (p. 78).

See checklist C8 on page 161.

Summing up

- Three things provide a basis for job satisfaction and effectiveness:
  - having well-defined, periodically reviewed roles and responsibilities;
  - having forums and channels of communication which provide encouragement, guidance and support;
  - having achievements acknowledged and communicated.

- A school's health and effectiveness depend less on there being communication 'downward' from managers to staff members, far more on consultation 'upward' to managers from staff members.

- Development depends on colleagues' having work that means something to them and so motivates them, and on their having conditions that enable them to grow through their work.

Reference

Herzberg, F., Paul, W. and Robertson, K. (1968) 'Job enrichment pays off: Five studies carried out in British companies show how this concept may be applied in furthering the attainment of business aims', *Harvard Business Review*, 46, 2: 61–78.

CHAPTER 17

Continuing to learn about teaching

Because there is limited time to take stock and think about how things might be done differently, you need to grasp opportunities to discuss ideas, make plans, trial changes and learn from your experiments. In this chapter, different ways of developing your teaching are explained. So too are ways of checking how beneficial your experiences of continuing professional development turn out to be.

How can you take charge of your continuing professional development?

It can happen that local and national administrations dictate that you use certain materials or methods. When they do that, they constrain your autonomous and local collaborative efforts to find what brings the best results for your pupils. But you and your colleagues can always subject prescribed and recommended ways of working to critical scrutiny. You can also refer and contribute to published evaluations of statutorily implemented policies and innovations, whatever their origins.

The daily, weekly, monthly, termly, yearly rounds of teaching can lead you and your colleagues to feel there is too little time to pause and think about how well you are doing and how you might do better. Take whatever opportunities you can to discuss your ideas with colleagues and others who have an interest. Involve teacher trainers and researchers in projects. Have an eye on publicising what you achieve and learn. It takes time and commitment to examine how effective your methods are, communicate openly, share perceptions, agree goals and approaches and continue learning.

Choosing when and with whom to trial a change is an important part of your decision-making. These are steps you can take:

- Think about what you would like to see happening less often and what you would like to see happening more often.

- Explore and plan ways of making changes to benefit your pupils' learning.

- Think about when it might be best to experiment: at what stage of the year and term: on what days of the week and at what time of day.

- Hold onto the idea that, if you cannot carry out your action research in ways that are well thought through and well supported, you might postpone it. If a project has to be shelved more than once, talk to mentors, managers and leaders about what can be done.

- Put into practice the ideas you think might develop your teaching and your pupils' learning.

- Examine what difference changes make, and collect positive and negative evidence.

- Compare notes with colleagues about how your trials work out and how to continue developing.

What kinds of continuing professional development might suit you?

Here is a list of activities that might help you, along with prompts to check their value and identify further steps.

Thinking about efforts to continue learning about teaching

Way of continuing professional development	When this worked well	Why it worked well	How to develop this
Working as pairs or small teams to plan lessons, study units and projects			
Co-teaching			
Carrying out 'learning walks', that is, seeing how well pupils learn outside your own setting, say, in other classrooms or schools			
Observing lessons and being observed			
Taking the role of learner in colleagues' lessons			
Looking together at examples of pupils' work, for example, moderating assessments and building portfolios of pupils' work			
Meeting to work on shared problems and issues			
Being coached/mentored and providing coaching/mentoring			

Continued

Discussing alternative practices: both formally, as in assessment moderation and training sessions, and informally

Sharing feelings about teaching and learning: for example, discussing aspirations/values/concerns and so on, with or without outsiders' facilitation

Carrying out personal or collaborative action research

Revising policy and responding to statutory or policy changes

Visiting and learning from other schools

Working with colleagues in networks, clusters or pyramids of schools

Engaging with professional groups, associations and higher education institutions

Studying for higher qualifications

One approach used by many schools is to facilitate meetings of interested staff members. You agree a focus, which may be, for example, ways of involving and motivating pupils, paired and group work, uses of new technology, formative assessment and so on. You share plans and experiences. You may visit one another's lessons, perhaps pairing up to observe and be observed. You can use your collaborations to go on to lead training sessions for wider audiences.

Some people give this kind of shared action research a structure, such as the one developed by Patricia Ashton *et al.* (1980). This involves each participating teacher once a week arranging to step back from the action of what is happening in a lesson in order to notice and note:

About your pupils	About yourself
What are my pupils actually doing?	*What was I doing before I stopped to reflect?*
What are they learning?	*What was I learning?*
How worthwhile is it?	*What do I intend to do now?*

Monthly or half-termly meetings can enable you and your colleagues to share observations and pursue implications. Those who have this kind of experience report that it makes a significant difference to their day-to-day work, their individual and collective morale and their approach to their personal and shared development.

Another obvious facility is physical and digital storing of resources in a library and on your school's intranet. TED (Technology, Entertainment, Design: www. ted.com) and YouTube (www.youtube.com) are obvious sources of teaching examples and ideas. You can also have access to up-to-date surveys of research, case studies and project reports. Andrew Pollard and the Teaching and Learning Programme are a rich mine of information (TLRP: www.tlrp.org). Excellent too are the Centre for Studies on Inclusive Education (www.csie.org.uk) and the Centre for the Use of Research and Evidence in Education (www.curee.co.uk).

Another pattern of development activity favoured by some schools is as follows. Periodically, a mentor or consultant provides a half day's collaboration with individual colleagues. This is one way of organising the experience:

An example of a protocol for mentors' or consultants' working with teachers and assistants

We involve in-school mentors and external consultants in the following process, the purpose of which is to confirm our good practice and indicate areas for possible research and experiment.

1. *A mentor or consultant visits a lesson or participates in a meeting or training activity run by a colleague. Afterwards, the colleague and the mentor or consultant have a meeting for between an hour-and-a-half and two hours.*

2. *The colleague expresses her or his view of the lesson or session, and the mentor or consultant gives some feedback. Together, they determine what questions and issues to discuss further.*

3. *The focus is on appreciating what is going well in the colleague's work and exploring whatever she or he feels would be worthwhile to explore further, perhaps, if it is feasible, with the consultant's or mentor's participation. The colleague makes a plan to follow up what emerges from the meeting, and, if it is appropriate and practical, asks the mentor or consultant to assist with ensuing activities.*

4. *If the colleague wishes, the mentor or consultant makes a record of the process and sends it to the colleague, who corrects any errors. If the colleague wishes or is asked to, she or he may pass it to a senior leader to document what took place.*

Here are examples of what has emerged from this kind of process in a number of schools, including Rowdeford School in Rowde, Wiltshire, the United Kingdom (UK).

Highlights in your lesson today:

- *Good relationships between your pupils, you and your assistant.*
- *Pace in moving the activity forward.*
- *Orienting your pupils to what has gone before and what lies ahead.*
- *A good balance between directed activity, which gave scope to your pupils' own preferences, initiatives, creativity, on the one hand; and self-determined activity, on the other hand, when they were able to develop their independence.*

Continued

> *You are choosing to focus next on trialling and evaluating ways of encouraging pupils to settle down better at the start of lessons and transition points.*
>
> *You are now going to work on how you and your colleagues transfer information between yourselves at the end of a year or other transition points.*
>
> *Colleagues are going to examine how to foster pupils' view of ability as something to be worked on and developed. You want to counter some pupils' apparent assumption that their abilities are innate and fixed.*

Another pattern of development was illustrated by the Slough Education Action Zone, directed by Frank Newhofer from 2000 to 2004 in Berkshire, UK (see John Blanchard, 2005). In one of the project's years, for example, fifteen teachers in ten schools (one special, three infant, two junior and four primary) applied for and were granted bursaries to support them in designing and pursuing research projects over the course of a school year. Two experienced teachers were appointed to work full-time across all of the schools, providing consistent, high-quality, flexible cover to release each of the enquiring teachers for approximately half a day per week. Here are examples of what some of the teachers chose to explore and their reflections on the experience.

Teachers' research questions

Is the combination of team teaching, demonstration lessons and lesson observations with feedback more effective as a training tool for the teaching staff than other training strategies?

How can we improve the development of our pupils' investigative skills in science?

How can we improve our pupils' parents' ability to use English and develop across the school the speaking and listening skills of pupils with English as an additional language?

Will teaching philosophy to children raise self-esteem, motivate learning and develop open-mindedness and the capacity to make decisions?

The teachers' evaluations of what they gained from the project

They reported that success depended on:

- release time being consistently provided by highly skilled teachers;
- discussions with a visiting tutor;
- having a time and place to work without interruption;
- having encouragement and relative freedom to explore self-chosen issues;
- having at least one other teacher to work with in the same school.

Teachers' answers to the question 'How has your enquiry project made you a better teacher?'

I have learned so much in only one year: how to research; how to improve my teaching; how to use what I've learned.

Time management: I am more organised, more relaxed, more flexible.

I can now see how to incorporate play in learning and see how learning through play is learning in a structured setting.

It has made me think about children's ownership of what they do and how important that is. The children weren't at first able to tell me what their targets were but, if they joined in the target-setting process, they can. It's no good having 'wallpaper' targets.

It's been good being able to put a new approach to staff based on my own trial-and-error experience of it. It has not been the usual case of telling them what to do by order.

I've had a shift in my approach to parents. I have become more challenging, putting forward their very important role. My previous approach was patronising. I now challenge them and ask, 'What are you going to do?'

It has highlighted for me some strategies for good questioning, for example, giving adequate thinking time (crucial for children with English as an additional language), second questioning/rephrasing and the importance of involving all children through the use of group dialogue, creating a community of enquiry.

It has helped me to help pupils do research projects, for example, deciding on structure and where to finish. You get to practise what you preach and face the challenge of producing practical materials to help staff see something tangible from the time you've had.

At the end of the year, the teachers came to shared conclusions about the project and gave their collective advice to colleagues and other schools considering this kind of action research.

When you have release time to research and develop your teaching

Discuss your plan fully with your headteacher and be clear about what you want to achieve: have an end in view.
Ensure the results will be useful to you and your school.
Set a time frame and, as far as possible, stick to it.
Get initial background information and guidance.
Make sure you have a facilitator, guide or sounding board.
Think outside the box.
Be prepared for things to change and go wrong.
Work on an issue that someone else is also working on.

Another opportunity for schools to promote cooperative professional development is their contributing to and taking some responsibility for teacher training. Training schools and schools that are centres for initial teacher training can be well placed to guide and support colleagues and trainees in carrying out enquiries and sharing their ideas.

An obvious follow-on from colleagues' having encouragement and opportunity to question and explore their work is pupils' having the same kinds of experience. Some of the most exciting work undertaken in imaginative schools is pupils' research into many aspects of school life (e.g. see Michael Fielding and Sara Bragg, 2003).

What difference do you want to make to your pupils' learning?

Here are some examples of developments you might be interested in, especially if you want to move toward your pupils' taking initiative in and responsibility for what they do:

What might you choose to work on?

To avoid ...	Whenever possible ...
Telling your pupils what to do	Help them decide what to do
Taking for granted that your pupils understand what they are aiming for	Help them have a sense of what they are doing by being shown how other people have gone about it
Taking for granted that your pupils understand criteria by which they are being assessed	Talk with them about how they can know and show how they are doing
Taking for granted your pupils are motivated and guided by their intentions and targets	Refer to their intentions and targets as a source of motivation, guidance and satisfaction
Leaving your pupils to wait for feedback	Enable your pupils to have feedback during their activities
Allowing little or no time for your pupils to respond to feedback they get	Give your pupils time and support to make practical use of their feedback
Assessing what your pupils have done at the end of a topic or unit	Make sure your pupils have much more feedback while they are working on a topic or unit than when they have finished it
Giving levels or grades to indicate your pupils' progress and achievement	Encourage your pupils to look back over their work, appreciate their progress and plan further activity and learning

See checklist C8 on page 160.

Summing up

- There are many ways of developing your teaching. It matters that you find ones that help you. Whatever in-service training opportunities you have, the crunch comes in your designing, carrying out and learning from changes you make in your lessons. Involving your pupils actively in such efforts can be very beneficial.

- Once you know what you want to change or experiment with and why, timing becomes important, as do consulting and working with colleagues.

- It helps if, early on, you define how you and others might judge the usefulness of your continuing professional development experiences and if you review your criteria.

References

Ashton, P., Hunt, P., Jones, S. and Watson, G. (1980) *Curriculum in Action: Practical Classroom Evaluation*. Buckingham, UK: Open University Press.

Blanchard, J. (2005) 'How far can a learning community go? CPD through teachers' enquiry', *Professional Development Today*, 8, 3: 5–12.

Fielding, M. and Bragg, S. (2003) *Students as Researchers: Making a Difference*. London, UK: Routledge/Falmer.

The Centre for Studies on Inclusive Education (n.d.) www.csie.org.uk.

The Centre for the Use of Research and Evidence in Education (n.d.) www.curee.co.uk.

The Teaching and Learning Research Programme (TLRP) (n.d.) www.tlrp.org.

CHAPTER 18

Observing lessons and being observed

'Observing' or 'visiting' applies to lessons as well as to other occasions when you and your colleagues open your work to view and comment in order to develop your teaching and your pupils' learning. This chapter gives examples of different kinds of lesson visiting and their potential benefits. A sample protocol is given, referring to boundaries and confidentiality; preparatory meeting; explicit agreements and arrangements; and post-event meeting, documentation and consequences. Prompts are given about how to evaluate and develop lesson visiting.

What are the intended benefits of making and receiving lesson visits?

This concerns how you and your colleagues can learn about teaching by visiting one another's lessons. It also applies to any occasions when you and your colleagues open any aspect of your work to view and comment. It can enable you and your colleagues to share experiences and perceptions. It is one of the most direct ways of promoting job satisfaction and morale, while potentially also informing shared agendas for development.

Benefits can include:

- encouragement and support in being reflective about your practice;
- immediate, constructive feedback and exploring possible ways forward;
- enhanced job satisfaction and motivation.

Who may carry out lesson visits?

Lesson visits can be made by a range of people carrying out a range of roles, for example:

- colleagues as part of professional development and action research;
- mentors, team and senior leaders.

In those cases, you can agree with your visitors how they will assist your continuing development. But lesson visits may have other agendas, for example, when your visitors are:

- representatives of your school's funding agencies;
- members of your governing body;
- certificating bodies and inspectors.

Why have a protocol, and what might it look like?

Because a variety of functions is served by lesson observations, it is important for there to be explicit protocols so that everyone can be clear and secure about purposes, boundaries, roles and responsibilities. Kibworth Primary School in Leicestershire, the United Kingdom (UK), was extremely helpful in clarifying these principles and practices in a project facilitated by Liz Worthen at Optimus Education.

A possible protocol for lesson visiting or peer observation

- *All observed lessons are confidential but, with the permission of the host teacher, notes and records can be stored and shared with others, for example, for purposes of ongoing professional development or external accountability.*
- *If questions of safety or capability are raised, the process comes under a different, potentially disciplinary protocol, and appropriate leaders or managers become involved.*
- *Time, place, focus and format are all negotiated and mutually agreed by the host teacher and visitors. When unannounced visits are made or authorised by the headteacher, the host teacher may agree or decline to view the experience as contributing to her or his development, and the remaining stages of this protocol might not be fulfilled.*
- *Where possible, teaching assistants are informed about and involved in preparations for lesson visits.*
- *The time and place for feedback are agreed and arranged for as soon after the lesson or event as is convenient for both teacher and visitors.*
- *The host teacher gives observers a brief plan and background notes for the lesson or event.*

Continued

- *Observers and the host teacher agree details about where the observers might sit; how much they might move around; what part, if any, they might take in activities; and so on, while recognising that the more conspicuous they are, the less 'natural' the lesson or event will be.*
- *With the host teacher's agreement, observers may use a pro-forma to record notes.*
- *At the end of the visit, visitors thank the host teacher and say something positive.*
- *During the feedback session, the host teacher is able to say how she or he felt the lesson or event went, and observers then have the opportunity to feed back thoughts that the host teacher can respond to.*
- *By the end of the discussion with the observers, the host teacher may summarise what she or he has gained from the experience. She or he may consider questions for reflection and areas for possible development.*
- *When it is thought useful by all concerned, a report of the meeting can be drafted and considered and, if everyone is in agreement, it can be finalised and co-signed.*
- *With the participants' permission, lesson visit records may be filed with a designated senior leader to be referred to by the teachers involved, the headteacher and senior leaders.*

How can you check lesson visits are useful for you?

You can use the following prompts to check arrangements in your team or school and learn about policy and practice elsewhere.

- What are the expressed purposes of lesson visits in your team or school?
- What evidence is there that you and your colleagues find lesson visits beneficial and productive?
- How well are purposes and protocols for lesson visits shared and evaluated?
- How can your experience of lesson visits be improved?

See checklist C9 on pages 161–2.

Summing up

- Visiting lessons can enable you and your colleagues to share experiences and perceptions. It is one of the most direct ways of promoting morale and job satisfaction, while also potentially informing shared agendas for development.
- Because a variety of functions is served by lesson visits, it is important to develop and update protocols so that everyone can understand purposes, boundaries, responsibilities and consequences.

Appraisal

Appraisal is defined as an official way of promoting professional, hence curriculum and school, development. It depends on cooperation between team leaders and teachers, teaching assistants or members of administrative or non-teaching staff. It provides a point of periodic, face-to-face contact and entails appraisers' observing appraisees in action. In this chapter, principles and practices are recommended. Qualities and skills that appraisees and appraisers can use and develop are outlined.

What is appraisal?

Appraisal in schools has the purpose of promoting professional, hence curriculum and collective, development through cooperation between an appraisee (teacher, teaching assistant, technician, administrative or non-teaching staff member) and an appraiser (supervisor, manager, leader or headteacher). More accurately, appraisal applies to everyone, including supervisors, managers, leaders and headteachers, who tend to be appraised by individuals who supervise, manage or lead them, either within the organisation or from outside.

In some education systems, such as in the United Kingdom (UK) at the time of writing this, appraisal is called *performance management*. A better term might be *work reviewing*, but *appraisal* is a word with currency in many professional and business spheres, denoting a cooperative, constructive process, so it seems sensible to call it that.

A possible definition for individuals' appraisal in school

1. *Appraisal seeks to promote individuals' professional development and whole-school improvement by facilitating consideration of appraisees' strengths and plans for maintaining and building on them.*

> 2. *Appraisal can relate to all aspects of personal and career development, and so can have a bearing on initial qualification, induction, threshold awards and promotion. For that reason, if for no other, appraisees' team leaders are well placed to be their appraisers.*
>
> 3. *Appraisal is separate from disciplinary procedures, investigations and inspections. It stops, and different protocols apply, if either the appraiser or appraisee decides that matters of health, safety or competence need to be addressed.*

Christopher Day (1988) spelt out how easily the value of lesson observations and appraisal can be reduced and wrecked by:

- having arrangements imposed without consultation;
- introducing procedures that are ambiguous, unrewarding or unpleasant;
- failing to take account of the time and commitment needed for reflection and development.

When appraisal works well, there are evident benefits, recognised by appraisers and appraisees alike:

> ## Potential benefits of effective appraisal
>
> - Appraisees and appraisers develop mutual respect and understanding.
> - Meetings produce decisions about successes, strengths, objectives and plans with practical consequences.
> - Colleagues appreciate their own and one another's achievements and are motivated to strive to continue developing.

There are technologies that can assist in this. The key is for these to be directed or co-directed by the intended beneficiaries. Systems such as IRIS Connect (www.irisconnect.co.uk) are designed to be a means for you to develop your teaching. But it can happen that misguided managers subvert to their own purposes of surveillance and control processes that have the potential to support professional development. If, as the appraisee, you do not share responsibility for how media and procedures are used in your appraisal, you lose the benefits.

Appraisal has the potential to be constructive, when the process:

- is negotiated by appraisees and appraisers together;
- confirms how important it is for everyone to have time and support for critical, collaborative refection;
- takes account of colleagues' concerns as they see them.

Who might the appraisers be?

These are some of the qualities and skills that appraisers need and can continue to develop:

- discretion and confidentiality;
- listening and questioning;
- confidence, tact, fairness and empathy;
- commitment to using the process to inform continuing professional development.

These are qualities associated with the role of team leader and typical of colleagues whom Alma Harris and Michelle Jones (2012) and Steve Munby and Michael Fullan (2016) refer to as 'leaders in the middle'. They carry a substantial teaching workload as well as responsibilities for one or more teams. Munby and Fullan describe them as personally humble yet ambitious for their school, honest, empathic, skilled, collaborative, courageous, passionate about their work, keen to agitate for systemic change, problem definers, solution designers, data literate, intelligent about whole-organisation reform, talented networkers and connectors of people and proficient team leaders (p. 11). These are qualities that appraisal at its best can help everyone develop.

Crucially, these leaders' influence is fed 'from below' by the teachers and other staff members they work with and in turn feeds 'upward' to senior colleagues and outward to partners, other organisations and wider communities.

What does a useful appraisal system look like?

Here is one way of arranging for appraisers and appraisees to have a voice in agreeing, evaluating and updating how they use appraisal to develop their work:

Example of an appraisal protocol

- *Our appraisal meetings have ring-fenced time and take place in an appropriate space.*
- *The appraisee checks her or his job description, previous appraisal records and any other relevant material. She or he completes her or his self-appraisal form, pointing to areas of achievement and development, and passes this to the appraiser.*
- *The appraiser reads the appraisee's self-appraisal form and reviews existing documentation for the appraisee, along with relevant data.*
- *The appraisee and appraiser have an initial discussion to agree timing and preparation for a lesson observation or work-in-action visit.*
- *The appraiser makes her or his visit to a lesson or other event run by the appraisee.*
- *The appraisee and appraiser have their meeting to agree:*

  - *a summary of successes and strengths in the appraisee's work;*
  - *a small number of ways in which she or he might plan further development;*
  - *how to complete records.*

Their conversation focuses on as wide a range of the appraisee's experiences and achievements as possible. The appraisee asks 'What can I do to build on my strengths?' The appraiser asks 'What might be done to help you do that?' Each offers their ideas and checks that they understand one another. Towards the end of their meeting, the appraisee and appraiser together sum up key points and agree for and about the appraisee 'What are your main areas of satisfaction and achievement?' and 'What will you aim to develop further, and how might you be helped in that?'

- *One of the appraisee's objectives relates to whole-school development, and at least one is the appraisee's choice for personal, professional development.*

See checklist C10 on page 162.

Summing up

- The appraisee and appraiser focus on promoting the appraisee's professional development, seeking to contribute to what the school provides for its pupils.
- Appraisal depends for its success on having the right conditions, agreed protocols and able people in the role of appraiser.
- Appraisal succeeds when it strengthens mutual respect between colleagues and motivates everyone to do their best for their pupils.

References

Day, C. (1988) 'The relevance and use of classroom research literature to the appraisal of teachers in classrooms: Issues of teacher learning and change', *Cambridge Journal of Education*, 18, 3: 333–346.

Harris, A. and Jones, M. (2012) *Managing to Lead?* Nottingham, UK: National College for School Leadership. www.nationalcollege.org.uk/cm-mc-let-op-harrisjones.pdf.

Munby, S. and Fullan, M. (2016) *Inside-Out and Downside-Up: How Leading from the Middle Has the Power to Transform Education Systems*. Reading, UK, and Thousand Oaks, CA: Education Development Trust and Motion Leadership.

CHAPTER 20

Using checklists

What an organisation achieves depends to a significant extent on how well decision-making is devolved to where the main action takes place. This chapter is about teams' having the knowledge and authority to do their job to the best of their ability. Ten checklists are given for key aspects of teaching. Whether they are called *checklists*, *protocols*, *standard procedures* or *key things to do*, they state succinctly what has to happen for work to be done safely and successfully. Their purpose is to enable everyone to be clear about best practice; to work together to solve simple, complicated and complex problems as they arise; and to refresh their understanding and skill.

What are checklists, and how might they help you?

In this book I have tried to explore factors that contribute to teachers' and schools' success, as explained by Pam Sammons, Josh Hillman and Peter Mortimore in their seminal work *Key Characteristics of Effective Schools: A Review of School Effectiveness Research* (1994). My intention has been to offer ways of achieving what Steve Munby and Michael Fullan (2016) have called 'connected autonomy':

> *There is no better way to build trust, develop capacity and increase collective accountability across schools than a robust peer review model, especially when the model has been developed by schools themselves … . Culture change lies at the heart of effective peer review, where the focus is not on the practice of peer review to 'prove' but to 'improve'. This requires a commitment to relationship building and the development of a culture … where the scrutiny of one another's practice, in a climate of enquiry and learning, is the goal'.*
>
> (p. 7)

Lazy, dishonest and oppressive practices have given checklists a bad name in some places. Ticking off items to 'prove' you do certain things diverts you from thinking about what you are aiming to achieve and how to develop your effectiveness. But Atul Gawande in *The Checklist Manifesto: How to Get Things Right* (2009) has shown how using a checklist process properly can save lives and money in surgery and medical care, building construction, aircraft piloting, space travel, food preparation, auditing and investment. The intention is to check the best of our knowledge and act on it carefully. This can happen at 'pause points' when we stop to run through a set of checks. To work well, the checks have to be specific, precise, short enough, easy to use and practical.

When teams focus on vital steps, every team member can revise her or his understanding of what needs to be done. This motivates and helps everyone to share awareness of what they do well and what might be improved. In an edition of BBC Radio 4's *Desert Island Discs* with Kirsty Young (11 December 2015), Atul Gawande said that what matters most is that you 'work as part of a good system and try to influence it for the better'. In many ways, his ideas are plain common sense, but it takes great determination on everyone's part to put them into practice: 'Groups of people working together are far better than the smartest, most experienced, most trained and hardest working individual in the system. If you aren't part of a whole group of people who are all pulling in the same direction, communicating with the same consciousness of what a good outcome is, you don't get anywhere.'

Checklists, used well, help you and your colleagues work well together and get more out of the experience. Teaching presents a mix of simple, complicated and complex situations. *Simple* situations can be responded to with prescribed methods or 'recipes', because mastering a few basic techniques brings a strong likelihood of success. *Complicated* situations throw up unanticipated difficulties and require many people and areas of expertise to be handled well. *Complex* situations are unique, so that expertise is valuable but not sufficient, and outcomes cannot be predicted with any certainty. Complex situations require systematic, collaborative checks to be made, so that high-quality performance can be defined, practised and, when necessary, developed spontaneously. In difficult and unforeseen circumstances, a person needs to be able to follow her or his own judgement and deviate from routines that have served her or him well up to that point.

A command-and-control paradigm may rescue an organisation from an emergency, but it does not help individuals or teams work well when their work poses ongoing, dynamic, unique challenges. Complexity makes it necessary to 'push the power of decision making out to the periphery and away from the centre. [People need] room to adapt, based on their experience and expertise. [They need to] talk to one another and take responsibility' (Gawande, 2009, p. 73). This involves individuals' and teams' taking personal and collective charge of what they do.

Summing up

- Checklists are based on known good practice and spell out concisely what individuals and teams have to do to do their jobs well.

- Checklists enable everyone who is involved in key tasks to share decision-making, methods and responsibility for their work.

- How satisfying and effective you are in your work depends on the routines your team has to use your knowledge and experience and so adapt to whatever circumstances you face.

What can checklists look like for key aspects of your work as a teacher?

Here are examples of checklists, C1–10:

C1. *To use checklists well*

- *We work hard as a team on defining essential steps and features in key processes, preferably no more than nine items per checklist.*

- *We work hard first to establish, and then to continue ensuring, that every person has an equal voice in making and using our checklists; no-one can ignore, belittle, overrule or silence anyone else who has a role in the front-line job.*

- *We use checklists not as recipes or prescriptions but as a tool for improving job satisfaction and effectiveness.*

- *We make wording straightforward and precise.*

- *We agree when to use checklists, for example, at the beginning of topics, units or projects.*

- *We systematically revise checklists, for example, spending a little time reviewing them whenever we use them as well as periodically away from the heat of action.*

C2. *To have good meetings*

- *We ask different people to act as chair so that the same person does not always have that role, which is to:*
  - *thank people for coming and check everyone has the agenda;*
  - *try to make sure the meeting achieves its purposes;*
  - *give everyone who wants to speak the chance to do so;*

   ° *encourage everyone to keep to the point;*

   ° *keep to time;*

   ° *check everyone understands what has been stated, discussed or decided, and what will happen next;*

   ° *thank everyone for having attended and thank individuals or teams for specific contributions.*

- *We have an agenda that makes clear whether each item is for (i) information-giving only, (ii) discussion or (iii) decisions to be made.*

- *We have varied activities, for example, talking in twos or threes before pooling ideas.*

- *We arrange to deal with questions or issues that are raised, but are not part of the agenda, somewhere else at another time.*

- *We get agreement on what to do if it seems the meeting cannot succeed or an item cannot successfully be concluded.*

- *We make sure everyone affirms their understanding of what has been stated, discussed or decided and what will happen next.*

C3. *To make good use of our pupils' views*

- *We try to involve all of our pupils in giving their views.*

- *We tell our pupils why we value their views and what we hope to do with what we find out. Then we keep them informed.*

- *When we consult them in relatively formal ways, we keep the promise that all statements will remain anonymous.*

- *We use a mix of methods to explore our pupils' views, for example, one-to-one conversation, group discussions, established forms of representation such as school council, working parties and perhaps questionnaires.*

C4. *To plan sequences of successful lessons*

- *We make clear, for our own sake at least, what we want our pupils to think about and what we want them to learn to do with their thinking.*

- *In the activities we plan, we state what we want our pupils to learn and make links with what they already know, what they are interested in and how they might use what they learn in other contexts and in the future.*

- *We plan varied activities that involve puzzles, imagination, cooperation, producing things and elements that are visual and physical as well as linguistic.*

- *We create opportunities for our pupils to understand and influence how their efforts will be assessed.*
- *We enable our pupils to have more feedback while they are working on a topic or unit than when they have finished it.*
- *We enable our pupils to look back over their progress and think about how to develop what they do.*

C5. *To have motivating lessons*

We help our pupils:

- *decide what to do;*
- *see what they are aiming for by being shown how other people do it;*
- *talk about what they are trying to do, what they are getting better at and how to improve their performance;*
- *talk about how they can deal with difficulties and mistakes;*
- *help and teach one another;*
- *use targets and criteria to guide them, improve their performance and sum up what they learn;*
- *get feedback as quickly as possible, for example, from one another;*
- *have time and back-up to act on their feedback.*

C6. *To make our pupils' feedback useful*

- *We help our pupils to see what they are aiming for and what they are trying to learn about or try to do.*
- *We arrange for feedback to be given and received during our pupils' activity or as close to it as possible.*
- *We make self- and peer assessment part of our pupils' feedback.*
- *We use feedback to pick out what our pupils have done well and are learning to do better, sometimes leading on to what they might now do differently.*
- *We check that feedback is responded to and, if appropriate, followed up.*

C7. *To have productive moderation meetings*

- *We use our discussions of pupils' activities to explore and clarify our teaching objectives, methods and effectiveness.*

- *We listen carefully to one another, explain our thinking as clearly as we can, question and challenge one another.*

- *We refer to relevant and published criteria to analyse our pupils' activities.*

- *We pay attention to what our pupils have done unaided, as a guide to their independent capabilities.*

- *We consider how our pupils' circumstances, attendance, attitudes, behaviours and other factors affect their achievements, but we focus ultimately on what they show themselves capable of for the purpose of making a judgement about levels or grades.*

- *Where possible, we compare our pupils' activities with examples that have been assessed by accredited authorities to fulfil specific criteria and represent certain levels or grades.*

- *We try to come to agreement as a group about our judgements.*

- *We draw out practical implications for our teaching and our pupils' learning.*

C8. *To enjoy professional and institutional development*

- *We engage in activities and projects specifically so that we can continue to learn about teaching and learning.*

- *Our pupils are involved, for example through school council and other forums and projects, in investigating and contributing to what happens in lessons and across our school.*

- *Our team leaders, professional development coordinators and senior leaders give prominence to research and enquiry.*

- *Our teams' and whole-school self-evaluation forms and development plans refer to colleagues' enquiry projects and accredited studies and show that research is helping to develop our pupils' experiences and outcomes.*

- *Our school has effective ways of disseminating in-house action research across our partnerships and beyond.*

C9. *To benefit from lesson observations and visits*

- *We all help develop our school's policy and protocol for lesson observations and visits.*

- *We develop our role as observers of one another's work, for example, by means of joint visiting, possibly supported by experienced colleagues and/ or external consultants.*

- *Visits are long enough to give insight into the hosts' ways of working.*
- *Both visiting and host colleagues agree aims, focuses and a timeline for the process.*
- *Provided it is agreed before the visit, and if it occurs naturally and does not rob the host colleague of overview and initiative, a visitor may join in part of the lesson or session.*
- *Both the host colleague and the visitor have copies of all paperwork and agreements.*

C10. *For appraisal to be useful*

- *To help the appraisee make her or his self-appraisal statement, she or he checks her or his job description, previous records and other relevant material.*
- *The appraiser reads the appraisee's self-appraisal statement and reviews the appraisee's existing documentation and related data.*
- *The appraisee and appraiser agree a time, place and agenda for their meeting.*
- *The appraisee and appraiser agree what steps need to be taken before their meeting: for example, timing for a lesson observation or work-in-action visit; what material they will refer to, with relevant permissions; and what measures or indicators they will use.*
- *The appraiser visits the appraisee's lesson or event as agreed.*
- *The appraisee and appraiser have their meeting to:*
  - *cover their agreed agenda;*
  - *agree a summary of strengths and successes in the appraisee's work;*
  - *agree a small number of ways in which satisfaction and effectiveness might be developed and explore how to plan for that;*
  - *agree how to complete records and carry out follow-up activities.*

References

Gawande, A. (2009) *The Checklist Manifesto: How to Get Things Right*. London, UK: Profile Books.

Munby, S. and Fullan, M. (2016) *Inside-Out and Downside-Up: How Leading from the Middle Has the Power to Transform Education Systems*. Reading, UK, and Thousand Oaks, CA: Education Development Trust and Motion Leadership.

Sammons, P., Hillman, J. and Mortimore, P. (1994) *Key Characteristics of Effective Schools: A Review of School Effectiveness Research*. London, UK: Office for Standards in Education (England); University of London, Institute of Education.

Young, K. (2015) *Desert Island Discs*, with Atul Gawande, BBC Radio 4. www.bbc.co.uk/programmes/b06r0vsn.CHAPTER 10

Useful websites

Award Scheme Development and Accreditation Network	asdan.org.uk
Birch Farm Nursery	www.birchfarm.co.uk
Centre for Studies on Inclusive Education	www.csie.org.uk
Centre for the Use of Research and Evidence in Education	www.curee.co.uk
Chris Watkins Publications	chriswatkins.net/publications
Computing at School	www.computingatschool.org.uk
Department for Education in the United Kingdom	www.gov.uk/government/organisations/department-for-education/services-information
Department for Education's extensive research archive	www.gov.uk/government/publications?departments%5B%5D=department-for-education&page=2
Education Development Trust	www.educationdevelopmenttrust.com
Education Survey & Research Service	http://www.edsrs.org.uk
Films for Learning	(i) www.makewav.es/thomashardyeschool/c/filmsforlearning (ii) www.youtube.com/user/filmsforlearning
Fisher Family Trust	www.fft.org.uk
Literacy, Using HOW2s and Visuals (DARTS: directed activities relating to texts)	https://teachinghow2s.com/blog/darts
The National College for School Leadership	www.nationalcollege.org.uk
National Foundation for Educational Research	www.nfer.ac.uk
The Royal Society for the Encouragement of the Arts 'Opening minds: Education for the 21st century'	thersa.org.uk
Teachers' Standards in the UK	www.gov.uk/government/publications/teachers-standards
The Teaching and Learning Programme (TLRP)	www.tlrp.org
Ted Talks (Technology, Entertainment, Design)	www.ted.com/talks
YouTube	www.youtube.com

Index 1
People and organisations

Index 1: People and organisations

Index 2
Themes and topics